with
one
accord
in one place

The Role of Prayer in the Early Church

ARMIN R. GESSWEIN

PrayerShop
Publishing

TERRE HAUTE, INDIANA

PrayerShop Publishing is the publishing arm of the Church Prayer Leaders Network. The Church Prayer Leaders Network exists to equip and inspire local churches and their prayer leaders in their desire to disciple their people in prayer and to become a "house of prayer for all nations." Its online store, prayershop.org, has more than 150 prayer resources available for purchase or download.

ISBN: 978-1-935012-58-0

1 2 3 4 5 | 2018 2017 2016 2015 2014

Contents

Foreword

It happened frequently. I would be working or engaged in conversation with someone when suddenly the door of my office would open, and a lean, dignified, rather tall American of German descent—then in his nineties—would march in, having done an "end run" around the receptionist and my secretary. In his hand would be a magazine article or a book that he knew would be of interest to me. He would stay for only a few moments.

"Who is that?" people would ask.

"*That,*" I would explain, "is Armin Gesswein, and he has executive privilege. He's been a dad in the Lord to me for a long time, and he's a very special person." This saint—a real man of God if ever there was one—had a name that was synonymous with prayer, having conducted prayer rallies for Billy Graham's crusades and established an organization known as Revival Prayer Fellowship, which has and continues to bring thousands of pastors and Christian leaders together in prayer.

How did Armin learn the importance of prayer?

Armin was a young Lutheran pastor, age twenty-four, striving to plant a church on Long Island, New York, and things were not going well. In his church fellowship was a retired blacksmith, about fifty years his senior. Armin had noticed that when this man prayed, things happened. Armin said, "The prayer and the answer were not far apart—in fact, they were moving along together. His 'prayer muscles' were extremely strong because of much exercise." Wanting to learn his spiritual secrets, Armin asked if he might join the old blacksmith in prayer.

Going to the blacksmith's home, they crossed the driveway and went to the old barn where they climbed up into the hayloft. Armin prayed. Then Ambrose Whaley, the old blacksmith, prayed.

Finally Armin turned to the old man and said, "You have some kind of a secret in praying. Would you mind sharing it with me?"

"Young man," said the old blacksmith, "learn to plead the promises of God." The old man had knelt between two bales of hay, and on each bale of hay was an open Bible. His two large hands, gnarled and toughened by years of hard labor, were open covering the pages of each Bible.

Armin learned his lesson well. "I learned more about prayer in that haymow," Armin reminisced, "than in all my years of schooling for the ministry."

The only heritage that Jesus left the church, he believed, was a prayer meeting. With Armin, prayer was not an appendage tacked onto a planning session or a business meeting. It was the main thing, the frontal assault. He was convinced that one of the reasons both churches and individuals are powerless and over-whelmed with spiritual impotence is that they have not learned the secret of praying, pleading the promises of God.

With the exception of his wife, I had the last meaningful conversation with Armin before he was felled by a stroke. With fervency he said, "Harold, we've got to get prayer back into our churches and schools (meaning Bible schools and seminaries)." What a man!

Understanding the relationship between the promises of God's Word and what we ask our heavenly Father to do has helped me immensely in my personal life. God honors His Word.

Learn a lesson from a man who constantly said, "Let's pray!" and he never meant some other time. He meant *now*! And then don't just pray, but pray standing upon the authority of God's word.

This book can redirect the focus of your prayer life, strength-en you with the might of the Holy Spirit, energize your church or study group and bring you into harmony with the will of our Father in heaven.

Ambrose Whaley's spiritual secret was lived out in the life of Armin Gesswein! It can be lived out in your life as well.

—Harold J. Sala

Founder and President of Guidelines International Mission Viejo, California

Preface

The church of our day has yet to discover the power of united prayer. We read about this kind of praying in the book of Acts. Armin Gesswein, author of this book, gives us great insight into why the early church in the book of Acts had so much favor and power resting upon it.

It was Armin who spent two years ministering in the great revival in Norway that began in the downtown Oslo Bethlehem Church in the early 1930s. This spiritual awakening lasted for nine years. When Armin returned home, he began an itinerate ministry, teaching and preaching on the importance of prayer and revival in churches and seminaries all across America.

At Armin's memorial service, March 2001, Dr. David Bryant, president of Proclaim Hope! said, "If ever there was an 'Apostle of Prayer' it was Armin. As you know, it was Armin's 'Ministers Prayer Gatherings' in Los Angeles that invited young Billy Graham to hold a Crusade in 1948—and the rest is history."

Armin and I knew each other for almost thirty years, ministering together in many churches and prayer conferences. I can still remember how often he would talk about the great revival in Norway. In one of his letters, he wrote this: "It was reported that in connection with the Bethlehem Congregation alone, about 20,000 people came to Christ. It was one of the greatest awakenings of this century, and it would take volumes to tell the whole story."

I remember him saying that if you want to get a clear vision about church evangelism and world missions, read and pray through the book of Acts. Jesus had no other plan except that little prayer meeting group of 120 in the upper room in Jerusalem that would turn the world upside down.

The secret is prayer.

—Rev. LaRue Goetz,
President Revival Prayer Fellowship

Introduction

Assembly-truth is the most powerful truth in the New Testament. Especially as it is on display in the Jerusalem congregation described in the book of Acts. I am surprised that more have not developed it. Once we get the idea that *church* (*ecclesia*) really means "*assembly*" we are off to the right start.

It leads right into revival truth of the highest kind. Not some kind of revival—but *church* renewal. We are introduced to the Bible basis of awakening for our congregations. This is the high road on which we find Christ at work building His New Testament church.

I finally understood it: *the local congregation is the basic unit for the powerful working of the Holy Spirit*. It gives new birth and power to all other action, whether it is individual or group action, evangelism or missions or witnessing or prayer or whatever. Move any of these into the action of an assembly and they move into another dimension of power, up to divine specifications. Normal. Mature.

BOOK OF THE CHURCH

The Acts has well been called the "book of the church." This is also true of the whole New Testament, including the book of the Revelation where the Lord says, "He that hath an ear, let him hear what the Spirit saith unto the *churches."* This He says seven times (Revelation 2-3). There is nothing like this in the entire Bible. When Jesus was here on earth, He would say, "Take heed how ye hear." Now, from heaven, He says, "Let him hear what the *Spirit* saith unto the churches." I earnestly pray for such an ear.

Lately I discovered that most of the things we are now seeking for our churches are demonstrated in the first church, the mother church, the model church, in Jerusalem. This tells me I am no longer merely in the realm of good ideas—but in God's Word. This not only gives us new vision but *faith* as we pray for our congregations. *Church truth begets church faith.* Now that "church growth" is the main topic of study everywhere, we must be very sure of our Biblical base.

Recently at a famous garden I stopped to admire a Mexican coral tree with its gnarled branches crisscrossing in every direction from the trunk. How like the Jerusalem congregation, I thought: organic in its growth all the way. Rugged. Tested. Tried. True. What a profound structure, branching out into all kinds of developments. One is reminded of the "tree of life" with its twelve kinds of fruit and the leaves of the tree "for the healing of the nations" (Revelation 22).

What a challenge—to trace the many forms of growth and life which came out of this one congregation! To take this assembly out of the Acts would be like lifting from the sky the very cloud which gave us the rain!

It is my prayer that God will use these pages to quicken churches everywhere.

—Armin R. Gesswein

San Juan Capistrano, California

December 2020- When they gathered in the upper room to pray and wait to hear from Jesus, they were under attack, banned from assembling, feared for their lives and the lives of their families. They met anyway because they trusted in Jesus and his power to help them and provide for them. They met in secret. (the believers) The stood on Jesus promise to meet them there!

In this past year of Covid pandemic, churches have closed doors in fear of the virus. I can't help but think; at such a time as this, isn't church power what is needed most?

CHAPTER ONE

The Jerusalem Congregation— Full of Surprises

This is a day of discovery. Not only are we going higher, we are digging deeper. By digging deeper at the same spot, archaeologists sometimes come up with some rare finds.

This is also often the case when we dig down again in the same Scriptures. Take, for example, the book of Acts. Many are digging there and are speaking and writing about the "early church."

There are many possible titles for this book. The simplest of all is *The Book of the Church.* We open it and there it is, *the church.* We also see Jesus at work, shaping it all up, building it.

When Jesus said He would build His church, He used the plain word *ecclesia,* well known in the Roman-Greek world. With it He at once brings us to the point. Scholars tell us the word means "assembly, congregation." This points out Christ's new plan: the gathered-people-of-God and their action in assembly.

In a nutshell, the definition is the action of God *in* and *with* and *on* and *through* His assembled people. It is so plain that we almost miss it: *assembly action.* This is now the dimension of God's power and working, and we must come to grips with it. We see it when we read chapter one of Acts.

Suddenly it is right there in full view. The Jerusalem church—the "first church."

We are in for many surprises when we visit this congregation. At least five are very striking. They arouse us into quite an awakening!

Surprise Number One:

It happened in Jerusalem, of all places!

We thought Jesus was through there. They crucified Him in Jerusalem. He said, "Your house is left unto you desolate." Jesus had finished with old Jerusalem; nothing more can happen there, we thought.

Would you believe it? Right there, in the hardest place in the world, He builds His church. *or at hard times!*

This fact should be a tremendous help to those who are at work seeking to plant churches in hard places. A fresh look at Acts 1:8 tells us there are plenty of these: "Jerusalem . . . all Judaea . . . Samaria . . . uttermost part of the earth." They were all hard places.

"This is a hard place," said a pastor when he met me at the plane. He did not know I had heard that also in the last place I had ministered. There are enough of these to go around!

Did you think it would have been like that?

Surprise Number Two:

It was a small congregation!

There were only "about an hundred and twenty" (Acts 1:15). Our first reaction could be: "Lord, is that all? What can You accomplish with such a 'little flock'? Is that the final result of Your earthly ministry?"

In fact, one might even be tempted to say, "Couldn't You do better than that?" Or, "What chance has a little group like that in so tough a city as Jerusalem? This doesn't look reasonable!"

It is indeed strange—in light of what we now know about today's churches, many with thousands of members. Yet many large congregations never awaken their communities for Christ.

Surely this should encourage any small congregation. There is no sin in starting small; the sin is in staying that way!

The point is, here was a congregation that really assembled! No member missed a meeting. It is rather ironic that this Jerusalem congregation, which was such a model in constant assembling, later drew God's earnest warnings in the letter to the Hebrews, not the least of which was not to forsake the assembling together "as the manner [habit] of some is" (10:25).

In the beginning and just after Pentecost, they never missed a meeting. Later they began to slip and members would skip meetings. By the time the book of Hebrews was written, members had made this a habit. They had forsaken not so much doctrine, but assembling. Hebrews flashes most of the warning signals for our present-day congregations—the danger points where backsliding sets in.

But the question lingers: *Did you think it would have been like that?*

Surprise Number Three:

How large that congregation became—and how powerful—and so suddenly!

All at once—in one day, the day of Pentecost—"about three thousand" people were converted and added to them as members. Would you believe it? We never in the world would have believed that if it were not written so plainly! And these were all Jews, mind you! Which adds to the miracle. What power!

Certainly there is some new and surprising arithmetic here! A 120-member congregation becomes a 3,120-member congregation in a single day. Every convert is accounted for and they all "stick." Instead of going off on tangents and in different directions, they all immediately become part of that Jerusalem congregation. And, what is more, they become like the first members. That is, they become the same kind of Christians, at once.

How can 120 members absorb three thousand new members? And in a single day?

This should answer a sensitive question being asked today as to which is better, a small or a large congregation. Here we have the story of a small congregation that suddenly became a large one. God evidently loves both.

Surely this is good news: God has a wonderful way of enlarging your congregation. And we must very prayerfully and diligently search the Scriptures to find that way.

Did you think it would have been like that?

Surprise Number Four:

The members all came from Galilee! A Jerusalem congregation, whose members were all from Galilee! "It just can't be," you say. But it was (see Acts 1:11; 2:7).

Galilee was a little over sixty miles north of Jerusalem. All these Galileans were now in Jerusalem. They were never very popular in the city of the great Temple. Their speech was poor. Their worship was not "pure."

The plot thickens! To think that our Lord would take those northern Galileans, plant them in old Jerusalem, and found His church with them! It looks like a first-class mistake: building a Jerusalem congregation out of Galileans, and right in the heart of Jerusalem, at that!

It just is not done that way! Or is it?

G. Campbell Morgan had a great saying about the book of Acts. He called it a record of "the glorious regularity of the irregular!"

Once again we must ask the question: Did you think it would have been like that?

Surprise Number Five:

Jesus builds a prayer meeting!

This could well be the greatest surprise of all! When Jesus builds His church He builds a praying congregation. Every single member was a praying member. A strong praying member. An intercessor. A real priest.

In this Jerusalem congregation we do not read of a "church within the church" (*ecclesiola in ecclesia*, as it is called). All the members were together. All were "with one accord in one place."

Nor do we read of "the church prayer meeting," as today. The church *was* the prayer meeting. The entire assembly was at prayer.

With us it is not like this. Most of us would not want to belong to a church which does not have a prayer meeting. Neither would we all want to go to prayer meeting. We now have "praying meeting members"* and other kinds of members, a sort of double standard of membership. And this is not being changed, not even challenged!

On the contrary, more than one good evangelical congregation is right now wondering what to do with the weak, sick prayer meeting. What is the answer?

If the prayer meeting were optional, we could simply forget it.

* and prayer teams, prayer committees, prayer groups

But it was not optional for these Jerusalem members. Voluntary, yes; optional, no, because Jesus had commanded them to stay in Jerusalem together. The word for "commanded" (Acts 1:4) is no easygoing word. It is a military term: He charged them. We must come to terms with this word of God.

A good part of the problem with the "dear old prayer meeting" is that we have not seen it as part of the doctrine of the church. That is where we are hurting today. We are low on "church truth." I mean not in the dispensational sense but in the plain and practical sense of the *ecclesia,* the assembly, the congregation.

This Jerusalem congregation furthered not only smaller "*koinonia* groups" (though I am sure they had plenty of these, too, for they went from "house to house"), but the entire congregation was a *koinonia* (fellowship).

A MODEL CONGREGATION

The fact is, this Jerusalem congregation, this "first church," this "mother church," is a model. And it challenges every phase of our assembly life today.

I have read portions of the book of Acts hundreds of times and some portions more than a thousand times. Finally it hit me: What is the story of this Jerusalem church? It is the story of one small praying congregation of about 120 members in an upper room in the city of Jerusalem which got on fire for God and went on to change the world!

That says it! What a revealing and revolutionary discovery!

If you were to ask me what is the greatest discovery I have made regarding the truth of the church, I would have to say it is this: When Jesus built the church, He built a praying congregation!

To put it even more plainly: When Jesus built the church He built a prayer meeting! This is the prime truth. The prayer meeting had priority in the Jerusalem congregation. We must rethink this whole matter with deep concern and with earnest prayer.

The penetrating question still is: Did you think it would have been like that?

Chapter Two

Kneeling Forms behind the Power

The Jerusalem congregation is not only the mother Christian church, it is God's model. God not only gives instructions for the building of the church, He makes sure that we have a pattern to go by.

Giving a pattern has always been part of God's unique plan. To Moses, He said, "Look that thou make them after their pattern, which was shewed thee in the mount" (Exodus 25:40). Later, Solomon built a temple according to God's design. In the New Testament, Jesus became the pattern. He is Tabernacle, Temple, Example—and more, our Saviour and Lord.

Then came the time for God's prize exhibit on earth—the church that Jesus said He would build. How would He build it? What would it look like? Where would it be? Where can we find answers? In the book of Acts, in God's Holy Book, we not only see that church, we can actually see Christ building it.

THE MASTER BUILDER

In chapter 1, the Builder goes to heaven, but before that we see Him putting together this new church—His most stupendous miracle on earth. He is following a plan all His own—a new plan. And when He ascended to heaven, He did not take the plan with Him; He left it here for us.

Moreover, He even left us a model—a full-size model, not a mini-model— in the famous upper room. It is in plain view: about 120 members, all praying together in a prayer meeting! Every member was present. Here is the crowning miracle of all Christ's earthly miracles—His new wonder in the world, the last thing He did on earth before He ascended to heaven.

In Acts, the Lord Jesus gave us not only a model, but also a blueprint for building. This is what we need to see and study. How we build up a church depends on how we read the blueprint. Here we have the "Book of the Church," the *ecclesia*, the assembly, the congregation. I must learn with Jesus how to build His assembly so that it turns out to be like His model. How is this to be done?

The model and the blueprint correspond. Our Lord builds a praying congregation in Jerusalem. His plan calls for a praying congregation to be the new vehicle for everything He has in mind. And it calls for us to be so much a part of such a congregation that we can never be the same again.

The plan calls for that Jerusalem praying congregation to dominate the book of Acts and to determine the course of the church.

Why does the prayer meeting have such priority? Why was it the first thing Jesus established when He built His church? When He left for heaven, why did He leave a praying congregation behind? Why was every member present there involved in "prayer and supplication"? What motivated all the new members—by the thousands—to become prayer meeting members, and to do so at once? How could they raise and uphold this kind of a standard for every member? To ask such questions is to ask God for some of His greatest secrets for our congregations.

Our Lord did not hide these secrets. They are written plainly in the blueprint He left so that we could work together with Him in building churches according to His plans. How exciting that we can be workers together with God!

And what a fellowship in the building! He is always the Master Builder—but He works in and with and through and for us, and *always according to His Word*. By His Holy Spirit He does it all from heaven. He watches over the blueprint of His Word ever so closely. Let us make sure we work according to His Word, too, as He did!

ASSEMBLY MEETINGS

It is very revealing and rewarding to note how many different assembly meetings are described in Acts. Look at some of them.

Chapter 1 is full. In chapter 2 we see the whole Jerusalem assembly on fire with its own kind of powerful action all day long. Then, in chapter 3, more assembly action and preaching hits us with full force and moves us right into chapter 4 with further high explosives from the same congregation. In chapter 5 we find ourselves in a very different kind of atmosphere, full of the awe of God and power of the rarest kind on earth.

Suddenly we attend two funerals, of a husband and a wife, all within the space of a few hours, and all of this in the midst of God's assembled people.

These are but a few highlights. In chapter 6 we see yet another kind of assembly action, and we can read on and on and find ourselves still in the glorious action of the risen Christ at work in building His Jerusalem congregation. Thank God for the tremendous potential of one small congregation of about 120 members!

The most important and strategic of all the assemblies recorded are the prayer meetings. Like powerful munitions, they appear at the most crucial times and win the day.

So powerful are they that the whole forward thrust of the church comes from them, as the thrust of a jumbo plane comes from its jets. Even before the day of the Jerusalem congregation the disciples had learned something about this. For the Lord had enjoined them to "pray . . . the Lord of the harvest, that he will send [thrust] forth labourers into his harvest."

Of all the many assemblies, the most power-packed are the prayer meetings. When the chips are down, when the battle is joined at the very gates of hell, the prayer meetings rise to the call of duty and take over. Like a mighty army of God, the church marches forward on its knees—on its witnessing feet, too, but its method is to take ground first on its knees, in prayer.

Observe a few examples. In chapter 1 the 120-member prayer meeting in the upper room is pregnant with "prayer and supplication," waiting to be delivered. Pentecost would celebrate a birth.

If we want to see how much power a great prayer meeting can unloose and set in motion, look into chapter 4. Notice that the original prayer meeting (chapter 1) did not weaken or thin out; the membership increased to many thousands! The prayer meeting increased as part of the "increase" (Acts 6:7). What a blueprint for our day when "church growth" is such a popular subject!

SIDE ACTIVITY? *It's true of all of our church too!*

Why do we feel a prayer meeting must always be a little side activity? Think of the prayer meetings that generated the mighty revivals in our nation's history. Think of the "American Pentecost" of 1857-58 when the nation became a nation of prayer. Think of the famous Jayne's Music Hall prayer meeting in Philadelphia where thousands gathered for prayer every noon, giving birth to revivals in churches all over that area. Think of the powerful prayer meetings which generated the movement of the Christian & Missionary Alliance.

Speaking on Acts 1:14, Dr. A. T. Pierson once said: "There never has been a revival but by such united supplicatory praying, and no revival has ever continued beyond the continuation of that same praying."

Most churches are said to fail because they do not generate their own power. This is also true of the individual Christian. Prayer is the generator. The great London preacher, Charles Spurgeon, once took some people down to his Metropolitan Tabernacle basement to show them his "power plant." There, on their knees, were about three hundred people praying for the service!

In Acts chapter 12 we see the Jerusalem church still praying at the same high upper-room level. Once again the battle is joined. Peter, their powerful leader, is to be executed. Why did they not call on just a few—the "prayer warriors, those in the church who really know how to pray and lay hold on God"? Because they *all* knew how! "Prayer was made *without ceasing* of the church unto God for him" (verse 5, italics mine). There was an all-night prayer meeting in Mary's house, where "many were gathered together praying" (verse 12). And Peter was delivered from prison and death by an angel!

That is not all. The angel also delivered Herod to death. But the prayer victory was even more far-reaching than that: "the word of God grew and multiplied" (verse 24).

No wonder the golden-mouthed Chrysostom once said, "God can refuse nothing to a praying congregation!"

Where have we failed? It seems that not only have we been ailing and failing—we have fallen. YES ⸮

First, our vision of the church has declined. This is primary. In practical language, our members place a low priority on strong and faithful assembling, though this is what the Lord really has in mind for His plan. People can miss meetings without any twinge of conscience. The book of Hebrews flashes the danger signals, and this is one of them: "Not forsaking the assembling of ourselves together, as the manner of some is; but exhorting one another; and so much the more, as ye see the day approaching" (10:25).

Today, we not only see the signs of His coming, we can actually "see the day approaching" (Hebrews 10:25). We should be assembling more faithfully, not less. God's Word here is a very earnest word.

Second, with that decline in assembling, the prayer meeting has also suffered. Instead of the prayer meeting being a concern for the entire assembly, it has often dwindled to the care of the few. It is generally considered to be an adjunct to the otherwise busy ministry work. This prayerless condition has now become so general that it is dreadfully specific—totally unlike the Jerusalem congregation!

Third, the Great Commission has also suffered and been weakened in this decline. The result is that we are heavy on the "Go ye" of the gospel but we are failing in other facets of it— without even seeming to be aware of it. The Great Commission includes many commissions—not just one. It is a command with many commandments. We need to see it whole.

We must "repair the breaches." God remedies spiritual ills by revival and renewal. Renewal comes at the point of the fall. God's call to repentance always brings us back to beginnings.

The blueprint shows that the Great Commission with all its varied commissions, like so much building material, was meant for the church God was building in Jerusalem. They will all be "fitly framed together . . . for an habitation of God through the Spirit." The church is the new abode of His glory, His new method for fulfilling His commissions—and the only creation having all the dimensions needed for worldwide evangelization. When we study the book of Acts, we see God's methods for fulfilling the Great Commission.

EVERYTHING DEPENDS ON PRAYER

Why a prayer meeting first? Because there is nothing in His church that does not depend on prayer! Its new abundant life, love, unity, purity, power, constant renewal, warfare, world evangelization, leaders, unending advance without defeat—all depend on praying.

If God is going to do it, it has to be by prayer. There is no other way! John Wesley recognized this when he said, "All God's works are done in believing prayer."

How did Jesus build every member of the Jerusalem congregation into the prayer meeting? The blueprint ties this action in with His Great Commission. He at once made prayer a total assembly action. But though the blueprint (The Acts) makes things so plain, we appear not to have seen it. Or else we do not know how to read it. Or have ignored it. Today we have a double standard for our members. We have prayer meeting members and another kind.

The Jerusalem congregation was not like this. All of them turned full circle from the Mount of Olives and headed right back to Jerusalem to form the first New Testament church prayer meeting in that upper room. Why? The blueprint makes it very plain: because Jesus commanded it! (See Acts 1:2, 4, 12-14.) He "charged" them (a military term of command), and they went.

They obeyed because they loved Jesus. He had said, "If ye love me, keep my commandments [plural]." And this was one of His commandments, one of the commissions of the Great Commission. "He that hath my commandments, and keepeth them, he it is that loveth me," Jesus said. Obedience quickens our pace to the prayer meeting. And it is the test of our love. I cannot say I love Jesus if I do not love His prayer meeting!

In Acts 1 we see all the leaders in that prayer meeting showing the way for other members. Today we have church leaders who never even darken the door of the prayer meeting! Unfortunately, many of our members are strong on the "missions" part of the Great Commission but do not sense the other facets or know the Bible basis and sanction for the congregational prayer meeting and its relation to missions.

The command for the church to pray is as much a part of the Great Commission as the command to "Go [with the gospel] . . . and teach all nations." It derives from the same blueprint. The Great Commission is built into His congregation organically, and prayer is the very lifeline of His new creation, the church. Prayer fellowship was the first form He gave to His new assembly in Jerusalem.

Dwight L. Moody once said, "Behind every work of God you will always find some kneeling form." The kneeling form in Jerusalem was the praying congregation—the prayer meeting.

"Lord, teach us to pray."

CHAPTER THREE

A Lesson in Unity

Pentecost ushered in a new day, a new era. But before moving too fast into the rushing, mighty winds of Pentecost, let us stop at Acts 2:1: "When the day of Pentecost was fully come, they were all with one accord in one place."

If we take this verse away we might as well forget the whole chapter. Like a watchtower, it holds a commanding view. It has a position of priority.

Ecumenicity—the promotion of worldwide Christian cooperation—has become a household word in our time. Books have been written and conferences and conventions of all kinds have been held in the quest for a basis of Christian unity. The first Jerusalem congregation gives us fresh insights into true ecumenicity. There we see an even greater unity than churchmen have been looking for.

SUPERNATURAL UNITY

What was the first great wonder on that day of wonders? Not supernatural power, but supernatural unity! Though less dramatic, this is as dynamic as any of the high-powered explosives demonstrated by the Holy Spirit on that day. It is the first miracle, without which the other miracles could not have been given in the way they were given on that great day: "they [about 120 members] were *all* [assembled] with *one accord* in *one* place." Dr. Joseph Parker said this is the greatest unity possible on earth.

Pentecost, then, introduces us not to the Holy Spirit as the first factor—with all the plenitude of His gifts and powers—but to the *church,* the new *ecclesia* (assembly, congregation). And the book of Acts consistently proves to be the "Book of the Church." The big surprise, however, is that the mighty happenings recorded here continue to be dominated largely by the Jerusalem congregation. This praying assembly is God's golden candlestick, His original lampstand. It lights up "church truth" like a beacon.

Pentecost does not begin with the outpouring of the Holy Spirit; it begins with a praying congregation. It is born in a prayer meeting. We must not lose sight of this. We simply must account for the fact that there is now a church in old Jerusalem, quite fully formed and fully functioning in powerful praying.

Why the church? Because God is not going to pour out His Spirit at random. He first makes a container ready. The new congregation is to be His new receptacle, His larger vessel, His agent not only for receiving the Holy Spirit but for fulfilling the Great Commission. He who had given the command "Go" now charg-

We've tried this on our own in our private prayer closets and have failed to experience this power of ch-

Yes

es, "Wait—don't go yet" (see Acts 1:4). He first forms and builds the church to embody all His action.

Too often people get "high" on the Holy Spirit but "low" on the church. People can run wild and loose on "Pentecost" if they are not centered strongly in the doctrine of the church. *Where you can see people getting off on spiritual tangents which may not be of the Holy Spirit.*

MASTER TRUTHS

The same thing is true regarding the doctrine of Christ. This is major. Along with Christ goes the church. These two, God has forever joined together; they are the master truths of the New Testament. Many other truths are there, but they move around these two: Christ in all His fullness and the church in all its fullness.

It would save a lot of headaches, heartaches, and church splits if we had as strong a view of the church as we claim to have of the power of the Holy Spirit.

We must emphasize: *The unifying Christian doctrine is not the doctrine of the Holy Spirit, but the doctrine of Christ.*

The truth of the Holy Spirit is not central in Christian doctrine. It was not then, and it is not now, a fact that is often learned the hard way, after various forms of sectarianism and schism. This often comes as a very sobering revelation to those who are drunk with the "new wine" of the Spirit.

If only Christ unites, nothing else should divide. But this is very difficult to learn, because any later ecstatic and high-powered experience in the Holy Spirit seems greater than one's earlier experience with Christ. The new "infilling" seems to make the former experience of the "new birth" rather tame by comparison.

Those to whom the Holy Spirit and "the baptism" now have taken first place do not admit this. They say that Christ is now more real and alive. But far too often a new sectarianism develops right here, with emphasis more on the Holy Spirit than on Christ.

The doctrine of Christ and the doctrine of the church are one. This is another checkpoint for testing splits. For example, it means I must not split a Christ-centered church or separate from it because I have been "filled with the Spirit." A sectarian spirit comes not from a new spirituality but from carnality. It is a work of the "flesh" (Galatians 5:17 ff.). (A congregation may also need to examine itself to see if it is dealing in love with any who have a new experience.)

CHRIST UNITES *committees, prayer teams leave out*

Only Christ unites and what is central in God's plan must never be secondary in our Christian experience or practice. One can never overemphasize the truth of Christ. "I can't get enough of Christ" is always the testimony of the greatest saints.

The Pentecost doctrine of the Holy Spirit did not unite the

120-member congregation in Jerusalem. They were already united! (See Acts 1:14; 2:1.) What or who brought that about? It was the risen Lord Jesus Christ Himself. After His resurrection Christ spent a period of forty days personally uniting His followers by uniting them to His Person. That was without doubt the most important forty-day period of ministry in all of His life on earth.

The doctrine of Christ is both deeper and simpler than the doctrine of the Holy Spirit, however ecstatic a person's experience. It is the only unifying doctrine, the unity already exists. It is ours from the time we receive Christ, God-given, not man-made. It can never be created at any ecclesiastical round table, however scholarly. It is a unity that comes by birth—*the new birth.* Unity pervaded the entire Jerusalem congregation. Christ was their unity.

How did all this happen? It goes back to Jesus' high priestly prayer in John 17. The more one ponders that tremendous prayer, the more he becomes aware that the Jerusalem congregation was the answer to that prayer.

Jesus' major concern was for "His own"—His future church. His prayer reveals the tremendous depth and range and reach of His heart and the immensity of His Person. It reaches into eternity and at the same time is plain and practical.

Christ's uniquely begotten life was to be begotten again in His church. Jesus used *organic,* rather than *organizational,* language in this prayer. He prayed for *oneness*—that the same kind of one-

when focus is on Jesus and congregation as one an there is less reason to look a single church member, who could disappoint or "fail" in some way.

ness that exists between the Father and Himself, that exists in the holy Trinity, would also exist in His new church. And we see the answers in Acts.

Jesus prayed for this oneness five times: (1) "that they may be *one*, as we are" (verse 11, italics mine); (2) "that they *all* may be *one*" (verse 21, italics mine); (3) "that they also may be *one in us*" (verse 21, italics mine); (4) "the *glory* . . . I have given them; . . . that they may be *one*" (verse 22, italics mine); and (5) "that they may be made *perfect in one*" (verse 23, italics mine).

Luke used another word to describe this oneness, one not used in the Scriptures before: *one accord* (Acts 2:1).

In Jerusalem, we see this new oneness at work for the first time in the prayer meeting. It is *assembly oneness*. It was in prayer that Jesus asked for it, and it was in a prayer meeting that it was first given.

For years I had a passion for discovering the secrets of true Christian unity. Then suddenly the inward eye began to see what the outward eye could not find. The Lord early led me to the development of a Ministers' Prayer Fellowship, where for years now we have experienced true ecumenicity, despite the fact that denominationally we are varied. The Lord has manifested His glory in our midst many times and has given us many renewal experiences. "This is true ecumenicity" is often heard at our gatherings.

There are plenty of differences among us, and if we dwelt on these we could have trouble in a hurry. But we have learned that these do not divide, because our unity does not lie there—it is *centered in Christ.* Christ unites.

Acts gives us the full answer to all five phases of Jesus' prayer for oneness. Five times He prayed for it; five times we find it answered: (1) in the congregational prayer meeting (1:14), (2) on the day of Pentecost (2:1), (3) in the ongoing life of the assembly (2:46), (4) again in a tremendous prayer meeting (4:24), and (5) after a judgment miracle of church discipline (5:12).

THE RESULTS OF UNITY

In His prayer (John 17), Jesus had also said that two unusual evangelistic results would come about through this same oneness: the "world" would come to *believe* and to *know* that the Father had sent Him. In Acts, the demonstration of the congregation's *koinonia* (fellowship) did just that! It proved to be a new way of evangelism. Moreover, it would even prove to be a kind of scientific approach.

Even the skeptic and the atheist would come to "know" the reality of Christ and Christianity from seeing this new, loving fellowship. "By this shall all men know that ye are my disciples, if ye have love one to another," said Jesus (John 13:35).

Thousands of members were added to the Jerusalem congregation. *Oneness* and *koinonia* accounted for the new evangelistic thrust the Holy Spirit gave to this assembly. That wonder contin-

Do we Hunger for spiritual experiences (highs) rather than Christ Unity.

ued at the heart of it all.

Later Satan tried to break up this oneness (Acts 5). He had so far not been able to stop the advance and growth of the congregation from the outside; so now he tried to do it from the inside. He did not have to attack their power, only their unity. But he failed again. Ananias and his wife, Sapphira, were both removed by an act of God. Great awe filled the entire congregation, and a tremendous new wave of Holy Spirit power followed. *The original oneness was kept*: "they were *all* with *one accord* in Solomon's porch" (verse 12 italics mine). People in Jerusalem were now afraid to join that church; and yet they had many new members (verse 14). *OR lack of spirit filled experiences?*

When will we learn this secret of unity? How many painful separations are brought about because Christians who have entered a new Spirit-filled experience shifted center from Christ to the Spirit. That is being "eccentric"—off-center. Christology—not pneumatology—unites. How many sad splits come about when Christians separate from Christians because of some strong experience of Spirit-infilling! It is spiritual pride that brings about the split—not the Spirit, not Christ, and not the church. The new Spirit-experience only brings this pride out into the open.

As we move along into the latter writings of the most prominent apostles—Peter, John, Paul—we see that their doctrine of Christ is preeminent. All else, including their earlier, more ecstatic, experiences in the Holy Spirit, recedes into the background. We are "complete in Him [Christ]," says Paul. John out-lived Peter and Paul by a whole generation, and for him the new birth seemed to loom larger all the time. This we see in 1 John.

For Peter, it is all *Christ*. For Paul, *Christ* is all and in all. For John, it is all *Christ* and our having been "begotten of God." That is the big miracle for him now, not "the baptism." And when he does speak of the Spirit, it is "the anointing," not "the baptism."

These men are God's mighty apostles. Our leaders. Our guides. Our examples. Our helpers in learning how to build and regulate congregations!

It seems to me that Dr. A. B. Simpson (the founder of the Christian & Missionary Alliance) was of this company. Who in our time ever centered and majored in Christ more than he? Indeed, he and his colleagues also ministered the Holy Spirit, with all His gifts and graces. Many and mighty were the out-pourings of God's Spirit on their assemblies. The Holy Spirit was not dishonored when they so magnified and honored Christ. They seemed to be able to minister the Spirit in such a way as to major in Christ and to magnify Him.

For them, Christ united. And what an assortment of col-leagues Dr. Simpson surrounded himself with! Men of various denominations met together in gatherings of all kinds. That is the meaning of "Alliance"! And was it not on such an "Alliance" that the Holy Spirit came? Was that not at the heart of the "fla-vor" so often spoken of about those meetings? These dear people could not get enough of *Christ*. They, too, found Him to be their "all in all."

THE HEARTBEAT

Koinonia was the heartbeat of this Jerusalem congregation. It was part of the new miracle of oneness. There was no Christian who was not a member, and no member who was an "island."

This *koinonia* life is carried out in two ways: when we are *assembled* and when we *leave the assembly* to continue in the same way in all of our living.

The total assembly can be lost sight of in the excitement of the new group movements: home Bible study groups, cells, "mini" churches, etc. The *entire congregation* is still the test, a help, a balance, and a corrective for anything else or less. We must not think that groups are the ultimate in power or the highest expression of *koinonia*. We must not settle for smaller groups, or mini churches. Healthy cells must be part of the larger organism—the body of the congregation. Otherwise such cells can turn out to be cancer cells!

I do not read of *koinonia* groups in Jerusalem. I am sure there were plenty of them—in the homes, synagogues, and elsewhere. Acts 2:46 implies this, along with other verses in Acts. What is explicit, however, is "the church," the total assembly. "The Lord added to *the church* daily such as should be saved" (verse 47, italics mine).

We are making progress today. Some churches have been finding fresh ways of making the entire assembly to be a *koinonia* fellowship (for instance, with "body life" meetings). The more groups or cells the better, *if* centered in Christ and in the congregation. They do indeed build up the life of the assembly and the action of the Holy Spirit there, and they can help to build up the entire assembly into a *koinonia.* Surely this was true in Jerusalem.

The famous "class meetings" were the secret strength of the great Methodist revival. They were the place for discipleship, training, prayer, instruction, discipline. But the great wonders took place in the larger assemblies. There it was that the Holy Spirit was poured out in mighty power.

God wants entire congregations to come alive and get on fire in the Holy Spirit.

This is the message of the book of Acts.

CHAPTER FOUR

A Powerhouse

Your church is too small!! (handwritten annotation)

It is simply enormous, and almost unbelievable, the amount of power the Holy Spirit can generate in one small praying congregation!

Nothing like this had ever happened before. Never had old Jerusalem been so shaken for God. Not only does it surpass all the other manifestations noted in Acts 2, it is the reason for them.

Everything on that great day is climaxed in the new church: *The congregation takes over!* All the action is church action. It leads us into the high New Testament revelation of the church, so needed and so much sought after in our time.

Today most believers just "go to church," not realizing that they *are* the church. They seem to comprehend very little about the assembly action of Christ and the Holy Spirit. This is true even of many who speak about Pentecost.

Pentecost is not simply the story of a new Peter, nor the account of any single member of the church being filled with the

Spirit. No member is an island. Not one is in isolation. It is the new day *of the church*.

There was no individualism on the day of Pentecost. The believers were assembled, all 120 of them, in one place (Acts 2:1). And they were "all filled [together] with the Holy Ghost" (verse 4).

If we were to take the congregation out of Acts 2 there would be no story. In fact, if we took the Jerusalem assembly out of Acts, we might as well forget about the book.

The more one digs into this book, the more one sees how indispensable this little congregation is, not only for this book but for the history of the entire world. This little congregation, which so soon became a very large congregation, dominates the book; Acts is largely the book of this Jerusalem congregation, because all the other churches came from this one.

MOTHER AND MODEL

This assembly in Jerusalem is both the mother of and the model for churches. Nearly everything we are now seeking by way of church renewal is to be found in this model.

Not every church that comes alive spiritually is necessarily a carbon copy of this one. Nevertheless, churches that are coming alive again—old and new—have certain things very much in common with it.

They have in common the things that pertain to life, such as Christ, the Scriptures, prayer, the Holy Spirit, worship, praise, love, fresh and vivid testimony. And all quickened by the discovery of *koinonia* (fellowship, sharing, joint participation) in a new way—yet in truth a way so old that it is new! We are experiencing what has been aptly called "the struggle of the renewed church struggling to be born."

Peter now is a new man—a churchman! He now heads and leads a congregation. Before this he had had many life-transforming experiences: He had gone from fisherman to disciple to evangelist to apostle. Now he is before us as shepherd, pastor, prophet, teacher.

Peter is as new at this life as the other believers are. They are all learning together. But he would now need every gift—and he had them all—in the new ministry *in* and *with* and *to* and *through* the church.

The church gave birth to a new Peter. The church is vastly greater than Peter, even in all his new charismatic fullness—as much greater as my body is greater than my mouth.

The travail of Christ and of the Holy Spirit is centered now in the congregation. This is the new way the risen Christ has chosen for doing His mighty work in the world.

The church accounted for Peter becoming a *new man* with a *new message*. There is also now a *new method*. We see it in the congregational action of the Holy Spirit. This is the dimension we so easily miss. We must learn much more about the corporate action of Pentecost.

The church is Christ's new creation, His new wonder in the world. And it has remained the greatest wonder in the world. Jesus said, "Upon this rock I will build my church; and the gates of hell shall not prevail against it" (Matthew 16:18). The church would be the most powerful force ever put into this world. It would have to be if the gates of hell were not able to prevail against it.

We find Exhibit A for all of this in Jerusalem, the place where they crucified Christ. The Holy Spirit now becomes a *church* doctrine. We simply must account for the fact that for the first time in New Testament history there is a *congregation*. This is the number one factor on the day of Pentecost—before the outpouring of the Spirit.

God did not pour out His Spirit at random or promiscuously. He had a new vessel ready in the congregation.

When talking of the Holy Spirit it is easy to get into dangers, excesses, extremes, to go off on tangents. It is the doctrine of the church that saves the doctrine of the Spirit from all kinds of fanaticism. The congregation was now the abode of Christ's glory (see Ephesians 3:21).

Many interpretations have developed around Pentecost and they all have their point. But it is strange that we so easily miss the *plain* and the *main thing*: that for the first time in the New

Testament one entire local congregation is filled with the Spirit and set on fire for God!

Fascinating! ALL AND EACH ✗✗✗

Indeed, there is double action here: a filling of the entire body and at the same time a filling of every member in it. *All* and *each*.

The attending phenomena also point to this. The rushing mighty wind filled *all* the house, the fiery tongues were first displayed as a unified, centralized flame, and then a tongue went from that to rest on each of the 120 members assembled. In that way, the Spirit galvanized the entire assembly for the most powerful demonstration ever put forth in old Jerusalem.

We are talking about a force that hit Jerusalem like a bomb! Einstein's famous formula says energy equals mass times the speed of light squared. Einstein showed that matter and energy are not distinct but can be changed into each other. Compare the amount of energy released by burning a pound of coal with that released by converting its mass to energy—the latter produces three billion times more energy. This is atomic energy.

Something like this is what we see at Pentecost. Pentecost is *mass energy*. The mass is the new assembly, which shows us an entirely new dimension of Holy Ghost power. This Spirit-filled church then hit the city like a bomb, and God cracked old Jerusalem open for Christ.

I say it reverently: Jesus did not do too much in Jerusalem in the days of His earthly life, though He went there regularly, especially at feast times. His main ministry and mighty works were in Galilee. But now He hit Jerusalem again, this time with capacity power. *Congregation power.*

Every congregation should experience this kind of power and should generate enough prayer power and Holy Spirit power to wake up its community for Christ. This is a new plan now in Jerusalem, and it is given, among other things, to bring us up to this kind of faith.

Pentecost, being assembly power, at once answers the question whether or not we are to expect revivals in our churches. Where else, if it is to be real revival and not something else or something less?

Here at Pentecost, we have the Bible basis and the Bible sanction for church or congregation revivals. With this God-given pattern, why should we settle for less?

Every member should now have a double kind of faith when he prays: a faith for his entire congregation to come alive corporately and a faith for every member in it. And we should not hesitate to pray in that order: from the body to the members, from the whole to the parts, from the greater to the lesser. The secret of all great revivals comes through right here in congregation power, because revival power is corporate power.

What about Peter's tremendous preaching on the day of

Pentecost? To *whom* does he preach? To the congregation? Yes and no. He really is preaching *through* and *with* the Spirit-filled congregation. The congregation is Peter's new force.

In fact, it is the congregation that preaches. The congregation is in charge. The congregation is the new witness, as a body. Witnessing, like the infilling, is also double: The entire body is a witness, as is every member in it. The congregation is "charismatic," endowed with gifts. This is different from singling out individuals and calling them "charismatics."

Power at Pentecost inheres in the church. "The Lord was adding to their number day by day those who were being saved" (Acts 2:47 NASB)—they were not added to Peter or to certain ones, but to the body. Just think of it: three thousand converted to Christ, all in a single day!

P. T. Forsyth articulates Pentecost's new order when he writes: "The one great preacher in history, I would contend, is the church. And the first business of the individual preacher is to enable the church to preach. Yet so that he is not its echo but its living voice, not the echo of its consciousness but the organ of its gospel.

"Either he gives the church utterance, or he gives it insight into the gospel he utters. He is to preach to the church from the gospel so that the church may preach the gospel to the world. He is to preach to the church that he also shall preach from the church."

Who is the evangelist at Pentecost? Peter, yes, but mainly the congregation. He and they form one body and sound one voice. Peter is not so much preaching to the congregation, but with them preaching to outsiders.

No one had put an ad in the *Jerusalem Gazette*: "Come and hear Peter, the great fisherman who walked on water!" He had not even preached for over fifty days. In fact, he had been completely backslidden. He had no time at Pentecost to prepare a sermon.

The *church* is the first factor at Pentecost. Peter first appears at verse 14 in Acts 2, and then as one of the congregation—*with* the congregation and *out from* the congregation. He gets to the outsiders by way of the insiders.

TWO SIDES TO REVIVAL

There are always these two sides to any revival in a congregation: get the insiders out and get the outsiders in! And how in the world can we expect the outsiders to come in to the meetings if our insiders do not go out? Here at Pentecost we see both sides and in that order.

Peter did not have to preach to a sluggish congregation. He did not have to pull them along like a big locomotive pulls a string of cars. They pulled *him* along. They even pulled the message out of him, and this is the way it is also in a real revival. Peter could not have done this on his own.

Such a congregation on fire does a tremendous new thing for us not only while we are in the meeting as a part of the action, but also as we go out from it, when we go to our homes or to our businesses or wherever.

There is nothing to compare with the quickening that can come to us in and through a powerful assembly, where God charges our entire being to capacity for Christ and does it in a hurry!

The same is true of a great prayer meeting. A person can feel very strong when praying alone but can be galvanized to tremendous capacity and immediate expectation for "great and mighty things" when praying with others of like mind. Nor is he any less an individual in this way. Indeed, he is more so. He finds himself and fulfills himself most fully at the same time.

D. L. Moody once was asked, "How can we have a revival?" He answered, "Build a big fire in the pulpit!" The wind of the Spirit usually blows from the pulpit to the pew. But at Pentecost the "sound of the rushing mighty wind" blew the other way: from the pew to the pulpit. And that continued to be the "prevailing wind."

I could covet this experience for every preacher! When the power of the Holy Spirit comes on a congregation and rests on it, as the Spirit came upon Jesus and remained, there is true revival. People are added to the congregation. The outsiders come in, and the insiders go out.

This is the pattern of the empowered congregation in Jerusalem.

The Jerusalem congregation sends us to our knees as we see what God can do with even *one* small praying congregation.

CHAPTER FIVE

The Revival We Need

S hall we see revival again in our land?

Many were asking this question when I returned from my first ministry in Norway's revivals, in 1937-38. The apostasy doctrine had taken over in many minds, the thinking that we were in the "last days," that the great falling away from the faith that was predicted had come and that few would be saved, as in Noah's day.

But, fresh from the fires of revival, my response was quick. "Yes, I *do* expect revivals, even in these 'last days,' God says, 'It shall come to pass in the last days, . . . will pour out of my Spirit upon all flesh . . .'" (Acts 2:17, italics mine).

New movements have come—the massive Billy Graham Crusades, for example—and as people started to see multitudes (not just a handful) come to Christ, the thinking changed. *Revival* again became an acceptable word. It even became popular.

But another question kept getting louder: Can we expect to see revivals in our *churches* again? My answer is, "Yes; where else?" We live in exciting times and the most exciting thing is to see God at work in many congregations. Many are coming alive in new ways now. Wonderful!

The Jerusalem congregation gives us the answer to this question. When it comes to revival, it has all the dimensions needed.

Albert Barnes, a contemporary of Charles G. Finney, experienced real revival. It was said the revivals under his ministry were not like brushfires, but more like strong, long-burning coal fires. In his *Notes on the New Testament,* he says that the book of Acts is

> . . . an inspired account of the character of true revivals of religion. It records the first revivals that occurred in the Christian church. The scene on the day of Pentecost was one of the most remarkable displays of divine power and mercy that the world has ever known. It is the true model of a revival of religion, and it is a demonstration that such scenes as have characterized our own age [1800s] are strictly in accordance with the spirit of the New Testament. . . .
>
> The human mind is prone to enthusiasm and fanaticism; and men might be disposed to pervert the gospel to scenes of wildfire, disorder and tumult . . . It is well, therefore, that there should be some record to which the church might always appeal as an infallible account of the proper effects of the gospel, some inspired standard to

which might be brought all excitements on the subject of religion. If they are in accordance with the first triumphs of the gospel, they are genuine; if not, they are false.

Barnes goes on to say:, "This book shows that *revivals of religion are to be expected in the church.* If they existed in the best and purest days of Christianity, they are to be expected now. If, by means of revivals, the Holy Spirit chose at first to bless the preaching of the truth, the same thing is to be expected now. If, in this way, the gospel was at first spread among the nations, then we are to infer that this will be the mode in which it will finally spread and triumph in the world."

RETURN TO NORMAL CHRISTIANITY

← This is normal—Not today's dead churches

The big question is: What is the revival we need? The revival we need is a return to normal New Testament Christianity as it was experienced in the Jerusalem congregation. That church presents to us God's normal pattern of church life—ongoing, not something pumped up or pepped up or stepped up by promotion. Rather, it gives us the normal, the standard for the church—not something special.

At Pentecost both the passing and the permanent were displayed. The passing was not the normal: the rushing mighty wind, the tongues of fire. What continued was the normal: A church membership filled with the Spirit, on fire for Christ, every member strong in prayer and in the prayer meetings, a power-filled, witnessing church. A congregation to which "the Lord added . . . daily those who were being saved" (NIV), one that "continued steadfastly in the apostles' doctrine . . . , and in breaking of bread, and in prayers." And one where the reverential awe of God rested over the assembly.

This is the day of the special and the specialist. We are all geared to this thinking, even in the church. We have "special meetings," and add on an "extra-special," a "super," and finally a "superduper." But the problem is that most all of our specials put together leave us below the New Testament norm; our "supers" still leave us superficial!

The special thing in old Jerusalem was the new church. Its members celebrated many special gifts of the Spirit, and its leaders were specialists. But all these specials functioned in what was the normal—a Spirit-filled church which had mothered them in the first place.

The Jerusalem congregation did not need the many "special" meetings we have. I am not against them; I am involved in them myself. But the Jerusalem church had a normal which was higher than our special. People were converted and "added to them" all the time.

They did not hold a series of special evangelistic meetings or depend on a special evangelist. Apart from Philip, one does not even read of evangelists. This is not to say they did not have them. But their evangelism was not *evangelist*-evangelism. It was *church*-evangelism, the strongest and deepest kind. Christ centered the Spirit's action in the congregation. It produced and re-produced converts "after its kind," so that the thousands added to it were all "of one accord." The Jerusalem congregation was indeed a "mother" congregation. The power of the Holy Spirit and the bringing forth of spiritual children took place within the congregation, the burdened, praying assembly.

We do not read of special revival meetings in the Jerusalem church. Their normal was better than that. Even when their preachers were in jail, the work continued as powerfully as ever. Why? Because the power was not only in the preacher or the pulpit but also in the pew. Because of this there was tremendous dimension of power in the pulpit as well.

What is the ministry of the evangelist in such a situation? Is the evangelist out of a job when a congregation becomes powerful in the Holy Spirit? Indeed not! He can then be at his best. An evangelist never functions so fully as when a church is "on the up."

THE NORMAL LIFE

I have often been asked about the Norway revivals, in which I ministered many times. One marked difference I saw was that they continued their meetings as a part of the *normal* life of the church, continuing them on and on, often for years, just as did the Jerusalem congregation. They were led to a starting time with an outside evangelist, but usually no closing date was set.

There was tremendous praying and expectation—and the spirit of revival was already there. The work did not *begin* with the evangelist but would often *break out* in his ministry. It had been born already in prayer.

When, for example, the noted Swedish evangelist Frank Mangs came to the Bethlehem congregation in downtown Oslo, the work had already begun in the church and was beginning to break. Mangs told me he was in another country, but could not rest—he was so burdened in prayer that he must go to Oslo. For years he had been invited to come, but now he came led by the Spirit.

Almost as soon as he started to preach, revival broke out. Soon it spread all around the city. No buildings were large enough for all who were crowding to the meetings—and they continued for *years*. For two years Mangs was hardly able to leave Oslo at all.

In connection with just that one congregation, no less than two thousand found Christ as Saviour and Lord. God's power was felt in the whole city— as in Jerusalem.

What about the messages in this awakening? They, like the meetings, were not so much "special" as the normal: the regular texts, the standard sermon subjects. The preaching seldom was long. Christ was preached in all His glory, with a major emphasis on His sin-atoning death and resurrection. His full Person was preached along with His full work. Powerful as the Holy Spirit was in His workings and manifestations, Christ was central. The regular means of grace were stepped up to New Testament normalcy. They were glorious and wholesome meetings, with little that was wild or extreme or fanatical. Much of the awakening took place within the framework of the Lutheran Church. (The Jerusalem church was, of course, still also part of the established Jewish structure.)

The work in Norway was not advanced by great promotional schemes or high-pressure methods. One looked in vain for spectacular or sensational ads in the papers. But reports often took over the front page and even the headlines!

It was not a healing revival, not a catharsis or a charismatic revival—although it was all of this. It was more: Like a tidal wave it came in on all.

There was reference to the full working of the Holy Spirit, and the gifts of the Spirit, but not one was singled out or put to the fore. They were all there, in use, but in balance, and Christ was the focus. The revival brought church renewal, church unity, church growth.

All types of converts were caught up with the gospel net. The risen Christ was at work filling it. It was not torn by church splits; instead, as in the case of the Jerusalem congregation, God Himself mended and wove it together into a continuous "one accord" condition. And the Lord continued to add to the church daily those who were being saved.

Everywhere, day and night, in the meetings and out of them, people came under conviction of sin. People of all ages and classes would be so convicted, at times, that they could not rest. They did not want to live, and they did not dare to die! Sometimes they would get up in the middle of the night and call for help. Some would walk a Norwegian mile (six or seven of our miles) to find someone who would pray for them and help them to find pardon and peace.

People who had not darkened the door of a church for years would come to the meetings, drawn there by the Spirit—people who otherwise were not moved or interested. When it is said that nowhere in the New Testament do we read of the unconverted being expected to come to church, but that the church is to go out to *them*, we need to be careful. In a great awakening, as in Norway or the Jerusalem congregation, *both* things happened. Never did the church become more *outgoing* and never did the unconverted become more *ingoing*. As at Pentecost, they came running together—the church was on fire!

The first problem is not to get the church to go *out*; it is to get all the *members* to come *in*. They are often hard and indifferent and drag their feet. How in the world can we expect outsiders to come if the insiders will not even come out to meetings?

Absenteeism was not a problem in the Jerusalem assembly.

On the day of Pentecost the members "were all with one accord in one place," and we read that "all that believed were together" (Acts 2:1, 44). They did not forsake the assembling together, as the habit of some is now (Hebrews 10:25).

We learned a lot about revival in Norway. Actually, what we saw there was not so much a special revival as what we see when we read about the Jerusalem church—*the normal.*

They did not even use the word *revival* in the movement in Norway. The word was *vekkelse*—"awakening." They expected the regular life of the church to be quickened and galvanized by the Spirit so that it would produce and reproduce all the time. Not a flash, but a constant burning, so that the light of Christ would remove the darkness from the surrounding community.

In the New Testament, it is the *church*—especially the local congregation—and not some kind of revival that is the major unit of the action of the Holy Spirit.

A good assembly—like a good jet engine—is meant for great altitude and for a strong, normal cruising speed. Many of our churches have "engine" problems. They lack power! The prayer life is so low that they do not even have enough prayer-thrust to get airborne!

We should not settle for anything less than normal New Testament churches! Was not this what Dr. A. B. Simpson sought and found? Was not the high-water mark of the Alliance movement the finding of a new life in Christ and His Spirit, which was to be the normal and as old as the New Testament?

Is not this the revival we need? God's Word calls us to our knees for it and gives us faith to expect it.

If AA can expect new "converts" to meet every day, surely we as a church can do no less.

They took care of each other, shared with each other and were there when someone knocked on the door seeking

They served meals too

Even as they were being persecuted and leaders were jailed.

Chapter Six

Model of Dynamic Church Growth

Ours has been called the age of church growth. This has become a major concern. The burning question we must settle is whether we want just any kind of growth or the kind exhibited by the Jerusalem congregation—organic growth.

Dr. A. W. Tozer defined the law of organic growth when he said, "Christianity will always reproduce after its kind." When God does something for the first time, we must look very closely into the action and not miss any of the details. Let us pursue this course with the Jerusalem church and watch for church growth in the first chapters of Acts.

It is very exciting to be introduced to the little company in the upper room (Acts 1).

JESUS' PLAN

Dear Lord, isn't there some mistake here? Couldn't You do better? All I can see there are 120 people! What in the world do You expect to accomplish with that little company? Especially in the city of Jerusalem, where they have just crucified You?

But Jesus said, "I've got news for you. Tremendous news! It will put your wildest dreams to shame: *I'm going to change the world through that little congregation!* I have spoken, and My Word is clear and plain and full and final—the last words I ever spoke on earth: 'Ye [you, *plural*] shall receive power . . . and ye [*plural*] shall be witnesses unto me both in Jerusalem, and in all Judaea, and in Samaria, and unto the uttermost part of the earth'" (see Acts 1:8).

But, Lord, I always thought this was a word for the individual Christian. Do I understand that You have in mind to empower the entire company?

Jesus: "Yes, I have in mind unique power, by My Spirit: *corporate* power for the congregation as a whole and *individual* power for every member. Waiting in one accord for that special empowerment, it will have all the dimensions for all the need. Capacity power, actually, for reaching a lost world. You see, I expect to reach the whole world through this new church. My plan is to build it in the hardest places, the very strongholds and citadels of Satan. Hell gates, really, like Jerusalem, all Judaea, Samaria, the mighty cities of the Roman Empire, even Rome itself. The church will be my superpower in the world, the greatest force I have ever put together because 'the gates of hell shall not prevail against it.'"

You will do all this through that one little church, Lord?

"Yes, through that one congregation. I am going to make it a *world church*, a church *of* all nations and *for* all nations; I have all authority in heaven and on earth, and in My risen life, I plan to go global. Come with Me now through these chapters of the Acts, and I will show you how I bring about this new wonder in the world."

At His invitation, I went with Him through Acts and was surprised at the way the growth came about.

I was surprised that a church so small could become a church so large! Big is not always better than small, and much is not always better than little. But normal cells must grow. Cellular expansion—that's the way.

I was surprised that the people were all Galileans. This is hard to believe: 120 people all the way from Galilee (some seventy miles north), planted in *Jerusalem*, in an upper room! (See Acts 1:11; 2:7.) Jews were suspect in Jerusalem. These Galilean Jews, built into a congregation in Jerusalem, are to reach Jerusalem Jews? Hopeless! Yes—but not impossible!

When these Galileans all started to follow Jesus, they had no idea that they would wind up in Jerusalem in the form of a *church*. Or that all Christ's great redeeming acts and truths would start and be centered there (His sufferings, passion, atoning death, resurrection, ascension).

Jesus moved His whole movement from Galilee, where He

had most of His ministry, up to Jerusalem, and made it the new center of gravity for everything (Luke 9:51ff.)

JESUS PROCLAIMED MESSIAH

Another surprise: On Pentecost, Jews from all over the Mediterranean world—thousands of them—were converted to the Messiah and joined these questionable Galileans and became one with them in the same congregation! Unheard of! When Peter preached Christ, many thousands were stabbed to the heart with conviction, they cried out and repented, and three thousand of them were converted—all on that same day.

This was the first time Jesus was ever proclaimed openly and explicitly to the unconverted Jews as the Messiah—and right in Jerusalem, where they crucified Him!

Think of it! Three thousand Jews openly converted to Christ as their Lord in one day, and it all came about through that one small 120-member assembly. It staggers my mind that these thousands were "added to them"—fused into *one* with them—though they came from almost every nation outside of Jerusalem.

I am surprised to learn, too, that the original miracle of being in "one accord" (*koinonia*, fellowship) on the part of the 120 members is there to stay, despite all this new mass and mixture (1:14; 2:1, 46; 4:24, 32; 5:12).

Koinonia *continued to be the deep, inner, organic secret and spiritual structure of this massive assembly.*

This Jerusalem congregation is poised to answer a recurring question: How large should a congregation become? As large, it would seem, as its organic oneness. As large as a tree planted by the rivers of water which brings forth its fruit in its season.

The book of Acts says "strangers of Rome, [both] Jews and proselytes" (2:10), became a living part of that church. That surprises me. The Lord took Rome to Jerusalem and planted Roman converts in that congregation. Later He took those Roman members from the Jerusalem congregation and planted them in Rome as a new congregation there. The last chapters of Acts tie right in with the Jerusalem church of its first chapters.

What divine wisdom—a world church is compacted together in Jerusalem for world impact. A whole world was planted there so it could in turn be planted in the whole world. "Whose seed is in itself" (Genesis 1).

SPIRITUAL MATH

This Jerusalem congregation also engages us in some astonishing arithmetic as it expands. There is *addition*, *multiplication*, and *subtraction*—but *no division!* What is even more striking is that these are all part of the growth pattern. It is organic growth, all the way.

First, *addition*: They counted the members and that first

counting took place in the prayer meeting! This hits us with a tough challenge. *We have lost the Jerusalem secret for getting all of our members into the prayer meeting.* It is not our piety that keeps us from counting our members in the prayer meeting—it is more related to pride. We play it safe! *Here we have the Bible sanction for counting our members in prayer fellowships and prayer meetings.* That is counting them where it counts!

When our Lord built the church, He built a prayer meeting. This has to be one of the greatest discoveries in the Bible.

Where is the church with a great prayer meeting today? Almost nowhere does the weakness of our congregations show up more than in our prayer meetings.

There are those who object to "numbering" the people. Not Jesus. In Acts we have His sanction for it: "There were added unto them about three thousand souls" (2:41).

These three thousand "continued" with them. That is a further miracle. They did more than sign cards—they signed in! They, too, became prayer meeting members right away. I do not know why we do not think about it, but in this Jerusalem congregation, they were really converts to the prayer meeting at Pentecost. We must again dig out the biblical secrets for building praying congregations. We seem to think this is optional, but it is not.

Somewhere along the line we have lost a big part of the doctrine of the church, for the prayer meeting belongs to the doctrine of the church. This comes clearly into focus in the Jerusalem congregation. It is not peripheral. It is the congregation at prayer.

It was to this praying, Spirit-empowered congregation that "the Lord added to the church daily those who were being saved" (Acts 2:47 NIV). To it ". . . believers were the more added to the Lord, multitudes both of men and women" (5:14). Here is a brand-new kind of evangelism—as new as this church. We are told they were *added to the Lord* and we are also told that the Lord added them *to the church*. Which is right? Both. Because the Lord and His church are *one*. They were married and had spiritual children. The increase is always organic.

MULTIPLICATION

Next, we hear of *multiplication*. This is the first thing we see on the day of Pentecost, when three thousand new members suddenly were added via multiplication: 120 times twenty-five equals three thousand. Does this mean that each of the 120 went out and won twenty-five people to the Messiah in those few hours, or does it mean that the power of the Holy Spirit energized that little assembly and stepped up its power twenty-five times? Something more like the latter, because that is what assembly power accomplishes. The power of *each* is stepped up by the corporate power of *all*. Why do we pray only for the

Lord "to anoint the preacher"? We should pray and believe Him to anoint and fill and empower the entire congregation. That is what happened at Pentecost.

Let us not lose sight of this continuing assembly power in Acts. The Holy Spirit is not only winning *converts*—He is building His *ecclesia* (church, assembly). It is the powerized assembly that He uses to produce and reproduce. *The assembly is always the basic unit for the action of the Holy Spirit.*

In this way, the multiplication continues: "The word of God increased; and the number of disciples multiplied in Jerusalem greatly; and a great company of the priests were obedient to the faith" (6:7).

Churches were multiplied as well as converts. "Then had the churches rest throughout all Judaea and Galilee and Samaria, and were edified; and walking in the fear of the Lord, and in the comfort of the Holy Ghost, were multiplied" (9:31). Who could have known that all of this would come about through one little praying church in Jerusalem, empowered by God's Spirit!

SUBTRACTION

There is also *subtraction* in the growth pattern of this congregation. We usually think of this as loss, but here it is gain. This assembly had two funerals (Acts 5). Ananias and his wife, Sapphira, were struck dead! Closer reading tells us that this took place when they were gathered. Who can measure the awesome power of a Spirit-filled assembly?

Church discipline is activated here for the first time. Ananias and Sapphira had "lied to the Holy Spirit." They posed as having given all, when they kept back a part of the money. Why do we not have church discipline today? Because we do not have this kind of power in our assemblies. It was after this cleansing that the reverential awe of God rested on this church and more miracles than ever took place and more members than ever were added. Even when the glory and fear of God were so strong that people did not dare to join (see Acts 5:13), more than ever were added to them (verse 14).

In Acts 7 we have another unusual subtraction, another first, in the martyrdom of Stephen. This turned out to be another case of new addition by subtraction: notably Saul, the fiery persecutor. The blood of Stephen cried out and turned Saul's boiling blood into a new channel. It was really this growing Jerusalem church that Saul sought to eradicate, only to find it breaking out in a many-sided new expansion! And Saul himself became a believer. The subtraction of Stephen resulted in the addition of Paul.

And what about *division*? There were no divisions in this congregation because they were all so deeply cemented in their "oneness" in Christ. "And the multitude of them that believed were of one heart and of one soul" (4:32). No church split was evidenced, because Christ united them *to* Himself and *by* Himself. They were added to the *Lord* and the *Lord* added them. When

God does the adding, why should anyone else divide?

Only the doctrine of Christ holds all of its diversities together in unity. *He* is our unifying center and life. Every other experiment for finding unity breaks down in one test or another. Only Christ creates *organic* unity. No church council or ecclesiastical body can bring it about. Stephen testified with his blood that no such body can take it away. Everyone who is born of the Spirit is "one" with everyone else born of Him.

Someone wrote the following:

> Because you belong to Christ
> You are akin to me;
> One in the bonds unbreakable
> Wrought for eternity.
> Spirit with spirit joined,
> Who can the ties undo—
> Binding the Christ within my heart
> Undo the Christ in you?

SATAN'S TARGET

The *oneness* of this congregation was Satan's big target. He tried to break it up both from *without* (chapters 3-4) and from *within* (chapter 5), but each attack failed, enlarged the membership, and increased the unity.

The Gospels record that Christ did make *one* division—but no more: "There was a division among the people *because of him*" (John 7:43, italics mine). This continues to be the way throughout the record of Acts. We are tempted to forget this when some new movement of the Spirit breaks in on the church. We can lose our moorings by seeking another unity center in "greater" Holy Spirit experiences. These seem to overshadow the new birth experience. They seem more wonderful. *But nothing is more miraculous than the new birth.* In it we find *new life in Christ.* We become *new creatures* (creation), members of His body, and members of one another. Any mountaintop experience—even the Transfiguration—leaves us at last with "Jesus only."

The *family* is also a vital part of the growth pattern. The organic growth of a healthy congregation can even explode into proliferation—something like grapes—in bunches. When Jesus spoke of "fruit," "much fruit," "more fruit," He had grapes in mind, the fruit of the vine, clusters. Entire households came to Christ—people like Cornelius and his household, the Philippian jailer and his household, Lydia and her household, Timothy and his mother and grandmother. Jesus chose a cluster when He selected the Twelve, another even larger one when He chose the seventy. The early church in Jerusalem made much of "household salvation," and many who read these words could give a similar testimony.

We dare not forget the *church at large* in this growth story, the entire Body of Christ. This phenomenon begins to unfold with the Jerusalem congregation, because almost imperceptibly this local congregation developed into the church at large. Every local assembly is likewise a part of this action. There are two bodies, each an organic entity and both organically related to the other. When I worship in a given assembly, I also worship with the whole Body of Christ on earth. We should grow in this consciousness as part of our own Christian growth. The apostle Paul prays that we may "*comprehend with all saints* what is the breadth, and length, and depth, and height; . . . filled with all the fullness of God" (Ephesians 3:18-19, italics mine).

This Jerusalem congregation produced many offspring. Yet in the larger development, the Christians continued to be "members one of another."

The church—like the human body—was self-sustaining, self-cleansing, self-supporting, self-propagating.

All the church expansion recorded in Acts leads back to this Jerusalem congregation—from the first period in Jerusalem (Acts 1:6-7) to expansion throughout Palestine (6:8-9:31), to extension largely through Peter's preaching after his conversation with Cornelius into Gentile territory, to Antioch (9:32-12:24), to Asia Minor embracing its first church council in Jerusalem, (Acts 12:25-16:5), to moving into Europe (16:6-19:20), and extending all the way to Rome (19:21-28:31).

That little congregation was a kind of international microcosm, an embryonic profile of the diversified world.

GROWTH FROM WITHIN

Growth from within is the basic principle of organic church growth. In Jerusalem they do not depart from this secret, even when the congregation involves itself in more and more organization. Organic growth was the inner secret of all its evangelistic outreach. It is always the Lord who adds to the church (2:47). Growth was not added to Peter or any other leader, but to the *church*. Pregnant in prayer and "with child" by the Holy Spirit, the congregation brought forth her own children and mothered them.

All *outside* growth comes through a healthy *inside* growth. The power of the Spirit at work out among the unconverted was in direct proportion to the power of the Spirit at work on the inside. The health and strength of the converts were in accord with the health and strength of the members. *Can't just be the pastor alone !!*

Some nagging questions are constantly popping up with regard to the evangelism of our day. Why, out of so many thousands who make "decisions for Christ," do so few become church members? They remain unattached and many cannot even be found. Where are they? Why are there so many spiritual orphans?

One answer is that churches are weak. Many are sickly, despite all the evangelism.

Many churches do not bring forth spiritual children because

there is no pregnancy! Spurgeon made much of this Scripture: "As soon as Zion *travailed*, she brought forth her children" (Isaiah 66:8). Where can we find the burdened praying and intercession which gave birth to the mighty revivals of the church? "The children are come to the birth, and there is not strength to bring forth" (Isaiah 37:3).

One preacher whose church was full of prayer was asked the secret of so many wonderful conversions. He replied, "We get them when we pray, and when I have preached, I simply call for my children and they come."

In D. L. Moody's later life, when many of the churches were weak and not a few had departed from the faith, he was asked, "What shall we do with the converts?" He replied, "Shall we put live chicks under a dead hen?" Get the message! The church is the "hen." When the hen is revived, it lays its own eggs, hatches its own chicks, and mothers them. The Jerusalem church was a vital, healthy mother—a childbearing congregation. To her and through her, thousands were born again.

EVANGELISM THEN VERSUS NOW

This points out the profound difference between the evangelism of that church and much of the evangelism now. They were added *to* the Lord and *by* the Lord—*to* the church because they were born *through* the church. It was "fruit that remained" (John 15:16).

"Operation Andrew" is a good illustration of this principle. It makes the greatest impact in the Billy Graham meetings because it activates and involves the churches in a unique way. In Operation Andrew, churches pray, plan, invite their own contacts, fill their own buses, bring them, and get real close on the way to the mass meetings. When any of these people make commitments under the preaching, they return home in the lap of the churches which brought them.

How much can be organized in evangelism? What about means, methods, media, techniques? Do we *build* or do we *plant* churches? How much is to be structured? Is it true that we organize in *evangelism* but not in *revival*? These are some questions that surface all the time.

Did Jesus organize? We hear it said, "Jesus never organized anything." Be very careful here. He certainly did use "means." He did not just feed the five thousand out of the blue. He organized the seating, then used a lad's five loaves and two small fishes. He did not always walk on water—He usually used a boat. He did not usually catch a fish with a coin in it to pay His taxes; He usually "raised" the finances in an orderly way not wholly unlike others did. In those days, when prominent women often supported a rabbi, women were organized as part of Jesus' tour and "ministered unto him of their substance" (Luke 8:3).

Jesus organized fully within the existing Jewish culture and religious structure, yet in full obedience to His Father. He organized the "big three"—Peter, James, and John. He organized the Twelve, and then the seventy. He organized a total in-depth evangelism program for all of Galilee. Later, He took the whole movement up to Jerusalem and built His new church and made it the new means for evangelizing the whole world. Jesus organized the most powerful organization in the world—the *church*, but He did it all the organic way—by prayer, the Word, the Holy Spirit, and in constant obedience to the Father's will. This was and is the most powerful way to organize. The organization grew out of and with the organism. It never killed it—only furthered it.

Too often organization kills organism. Dr. Vance Havner aptly depicts what happens: first we have a *man* and a *message*, then a *movement*, and in the end a *monument.*

Jeremiah used the words "to *build* and to *plant*" (Jeremiah 1:10; 31:28, italics mine). The church must be built and this envisions planning, organization, methods, and structuring. "No relationship of love can develop unless there are structures in which it can grow," says one leader. Charles G. Finney insisted that we must use means and measures in reaching for results. He spoke of "promoting revivals." The means should be those adapted to the ends desired.

Finney also said that "the idea that God ordinarily works independently of human instrumentality, or without reference to the adaptation of means to ends, is unscriptural." He even went so far as to say that to expect results without the use of God-given means is a form of fanaticism.

Promoting evangelism can be spiritual. It is like the use of money—it is all spiritual if we are spiritual. All organization, methods, techniques, etc., are good only if the dynamic of the Spirit is at work with them. Jesus said, "By this shall all men know that ye are my disciples, if ye have love one to another" (John 13:35). This is the best dynamic and we are learning more about it today in formations of *koinonia* groups.

I am more convinced than ever that *koinonia* (one accord fellowship) is the divine principle of healthy evangelism and all church growth. Andrew Murray wrote: "In the church of Christ we have not merely 'one Spirit' but 'one body' and *everything that tends to emphasize the unity of the body brings a blessing with it*" (italics mine).

One of my pastor friends adheres closely to this principle and it dominates and determines action in his board meetings. If a matter comes up about which there is disagreement, they table it for further prayer until they come to full agreement. This kind of oneness among the leaders permeates the entire congregation, which is growing stronger and larger all the time. Jesus prayed "that they *all* may be *one* . . . that the world may *believe* . . . and . . . may *know*" (John 17:21, 23, italics mine).

Christ prayed this new dynamic into being. In the book of Acts we see the answer. There we witness this kind of evangelism and growth embodied in the Jerusalem congregation. It is God's model of dynamic church growth, His supreme wonder in the world!

But we must remember: it is difficult to win *to* the church those not won *through* the church.

CHAPTER SEVEN

Social Action

Social Action . . . Social Gospel . . . Living Redemptively.
Are these signals for controversy, or are they matters of conscience? Are they red flags or banners?

Do we "cop out" here? Do we leave the alcoholics to Alcoholics Anonymous? The drug addicts to the "Jesus freaks"? Do we depend on the Salvation Army or the Volunteers of America for all the social help?

Now that government has taken over most of the welfare and we are virtually a welfare state, what do we do? Is the church no longer called or needed to help the needy? Do we just preach the gospel or do we also get our hands dirty?

How much should happen through a congregation? First on the inside, in the "community of God," then on the outside, in the surrounding community? First in the household of faith, then in other households?

THE BIBLE AND THE POOR

The Bible certainly has a lot to say about the "poor and needy."
The Old Testament law required specific sacrifices for the poor
and merciful action for all the needy. The New Testament says
God is the Father of the fatherless and the Husband of the widow.
In our day, the "social" aspect of our faith has become an area
of confusion, frustration, and even controversy for evangelical
churches.

John the Baptist "came preaching." He had a lot to *say* to all
classes and levels of society, including publicans and soldiers. But
he pursued no social action.

Jesus did much more. It takes but a casual reading of the Gospels
to see that Christ went to work on the *total man* and the *totality of
mankind.* He entered the heart of humanity incarnationally. "The
Word became flesh and dwelt among us." He surprised everyone. In His hometown synagogue at Nazareth, He openly an-
nounced the Magna Carta of His forthcoming ministry in all its
dimensions: "The Spirit of the Lord is upon me, because he hath
anointed me to preach the gospel to the poor; he hath sent me
to heal the brokenhearted, to preach deliverance to the captives,
and recovering of sight to the blind, to set at liberty them that are
bruised, to preach the acceptable year of the Lord" (Luke 4:18-19).

Palestine was an overcrowded land, full of poverty and hunger; a land of poor resources and want. It was unsafe to travel.
Thieves and murderers were all around. Need was everywhere.

Jesus saw all this as a potential harvest. He taught us to "call the poor, the maimed, the lame, and the blind." He said we are to give the hungry something to eat, the thirsty a drink. We are to invite strangers into our homes, give clothes to them who have none, visit the sick and those in prison. Yes, even give a cup of cold water in His name (Matthew 25:31-46).

Jesus did not only preach and "win souls." He healed all kinds of broken bodies and fed needy people. Many publicans and harlots and outcasts found in Him a kind of "city of refuge." He had a solution for every strata of society. When in prison, John the Baptist began to doubt whether Jesus really was the Messiah. Jesus reassured him with the message: ". . . the blind receive their sight, and the lame walk, the lepers are cleansed, and the deaf hear, the dead are raised up, and the poor have the gospel preached unto them" (Matthew 11:5).

Christ walked the same streets as the outcasts; He ate with all kinds of "sinners." He lifted the bruised and crushed. He suffered for the suffering. He made the lame to leap and the dumb to sing. He ministered to every man and to every need. He offered help as "far as the curse is found."

If we read the Gospels without theological bias or prejudice, we see that Jesus gave almost as much time and attention to the *bodies* of people as to their *souls.*

Both the vertical and the horizontal are central in the life of Christ. Two beams made up His cross and they pinpoint the two directions of His life. The one reaches up to His Father, the other out to men. His power was vertical—His ministry was horizontal. His feet were nailed (or tied) to the vertical beam; His walk was "from above" and always pleasing to the Father. His hands were nailed to the horizontal beam; with those hands He blessed little children and multiplied loaves and fishes for the hungry. He touched the sick and the blind. He never did anything but good—and was crucified for it!

When Jesus ascended to heaven, He made His church to be His new body on earth, the body in which He could live again and continue His life and work on earth.

On the Jericho road, the Good Samaritan did not just give the robbed, stripped, bleeding man a gospel tract! (The priest and the Levite did not even do that much.) He got involved and took on the responsibility for the man's full care and cure. Jesus says to us: "Go and do thou likewise."

At the beginning of my pastoral ministry, I used to help the poor and even got some of them to come to my church. Some I won for Christ; some I did not. A few of my members criticized me for doing this. In another church, I helped some "down and outers" and started a work among blacks, but some of the prominent people in the congregation tried to talk me out of that. These efforts, I grant, were not much. But they were beginnings.

James, our Lord's half-brother and head of the Jerusalem congregation, wrote: "If you have a friend who is in need of food and clothing, and you say to him, 'Well, good-bye and God bless you; stay warm and eat hearty,' and then don't give him clothes or food, what good does that do?" (James 2:15-16, TLB).

MAN'S TOTAL NEED

This does not mean that the church is to provide full employment and feed all the poor and clean out all the moral rot in the neighborhood; it does not mean the church must solve all the gnawing problems of human rights and race or provide homes for all the homeless and hopeless refugees. It does mean the church is to be involved in man's *total* need, *redemptively*, through Christ.

John, the apostle of love, who lived a whole generation after Peter and Paul were martyred, the only apostle who had a three-generation ministry, wrote in his later years: "If someone who is supposed to be a Christian has money enough to live well, and sees a brother in need, and won't help him—how can God's love be within him? Little children, let us stop just *saying* we love people; let us *really* love them, and *show it by our actions*" (1 John 3:17-18, italics mine, TLB).

The church, as Dr. John Stott says, must learn the secret of community. Therein lies the secret of its communication, its lifeline. The church is a community, social in action.

The church is not only salt, staying corruption. It is not only light, dispelling darkness. It is *life* and *life-giving*.

Corporate life always affects other corporate life. The church is a society within a society, for its redemption. It lives in the community socially. Just as Christ was one with the people He came to save, so the congregation makes common cause with its neighborhood. There is an affinity as well as much that is reciprocal, exchange and interaction. Every area of interaction can become ground for seeding and propagation.

A good part of the community should come alive in its church. The Corinthian congregation certainly opens this up to our view. We can visualize the church in Corinth, as well as Corinth in the church, for Paul speaks of fornicators, idolaters, adulterers, effeminate, abusers of themselves with mankind (homosexuals), thieves, covetous, drunkards, revilers (slanderers), extortioners (swindlers). That is, they *were* such, but they are now "washed . . . sanctified, . . . justified in the name of the Lord Jesus, and by the Spirit of our God" (1 Corinthians 6:9–11). That change took a lot of power! When Paul came to a city his gospel "came not in word only, but also in power, and in the Holy Spirit, and in much assurance" (1 Thessalonians 1:5). Paul and his helpers ministered that way in Corinth for a year and a half, for God made it clear to him that He had "much people in this city" (Acts 18:10).

In Jerusalem, the church shows the way into community action because it was a community and demonstrated full community action within itself. Like a prism, this congregation manifested the multicolored splendor of Christ in many directions. It related not only to the many sins of the community but also to its many needs. Jesus helped the oppressed and the suppressed and the depressed. He embraced robbers, harlots, Samaritans, and Gentiles—the church takes them in after converting them. Many are its converts and many are the moral changes—even when all are not converted.

BY-PRODUCTS

Who can list all the by-products that come in the wake of a strong congregation?

Converted alcoholics are burdened for other alcoholics. Young people relate to other young people, children relate to children. Empowered by the assembly, they reach many of their kind. We share a common life in Christ as Christians and a common life in the community as humans. Something of the community lives in every person in it.

"Bloom where you are planted," says a gospel tract. Every plant has in it elements of its own soil. Like a tree which roots itself in its own soil, so the church draws on Christ and turns back much of its own life to the community in fruit for God. A church that does not reach out will soon die.

Edward Markham said of Abraham Lincoln: "The color of the ground was in him, the red earth, the smack and tang of elemental things." How true this is of Christ, and it must be of His church also. Drugs, alcoholism, prostitution, poverty, race, crime, prisons, hunger, pornography, education, and the political arena—these are all the burden of Christ, and therefore of the church. He is the silver lining for every black cloud in society. An organic field, we are told, surrounds an organic body, an energy aura, a kind of dynamic area of energy exchange. This certainly is true of a Spirit-charged organism like the church in Jerusalem, the example for us.

A congregation also reflects something of the culture and personality of its community. The "species" vary a lot. Witness, for example, the seven churches of the Revelation (see Revelation 1-3). They were all "apostolic" congregations, and yet how diverse were they in personality and development. Each church reflected the surrounding society within its own society.

In Pergamos, for example, where "Satan's seat" was, the church battled its own kind of sins, and these same sins were coloring it as a congregation. The church in this kind of a world was letting its world get on its inside (see Revelation 3:12ff.).

Because a church is socially oriented, it sparks more than personal evangelism. There is bound to be a living, organic, and social interaction where it is rooted.

In Jerusalem, Peter did not just stand on a soap box on a corner and preach. He ministered in and with and through a very social structure—the congregation. That church was propagating, not only the gospel, but its very own life. Organic life was now begetting organic life, even in the very city where Christ was crucified!

From the day of Pentecost on, this church began to operate *as a community within a community.* Organized evil was rooted in the structures of society. Christ now counters all that by converting a lot of it to His own new society. Every such evil affords Him a new point of contact. In "church planting," this is a major factor, and our faith must move in with Christ.

We often hear it said, "Evangelism is the cutting edge of the church." In Jerusalem, the process was reversed. *The congregation became the new cutting edge for evangelism.* The chicken is before the egg! The new *koinonia* and oneness and love expressed in this new assembly become evangelistic—powerfully so—and in a new way, as Jesus said they would: "By this shall all men know . . . if ye have love one to another" (John 13:35). "I pray . . . that they all may be one . . . that the world may *believe* . . . and *know*" (John 17:21-23). Jesus here prayed a new evangelism into being— *church born and church borne.*

Acts 1:8 tells us the same thing. We must read what Jesus actually said. The parting word of Jesus is the key verse of the Acts: "*Ye* shall receive power, after that the Holy Spirit is come upon you: and *ye* shall be witnesses unto me both in Jerusalem, and in all Judaea, and in Samaria, and unto the uttermost part of the earth" (italics mine). It is very easy to miss the two *ye's* (plural) and the four *ands*—all spoken to the same company of Galileans who saw Jesus go to heaven.

MORE THAN PERSONAL POWER

What does all this mean? Jesus here promises much more than *personal* power for *personal* witnessing, though that is included. He outlines the power and progress of a *congregation*, the Jerusalem assembly. How strange that we so easily miss what He actually said. The Galilean followers who returned from the mount of His ascension to Jerusalem and the upper room became His first church. This is without question one of the greatest turns in the road recorded in the Bible. Jesus had commanded them to do this (see Acts 1:4). By His power that one little congregation would live to fulfill everything spoken of in verse 8. Who would have dared to believe that one small assembly would change the world! That is the story of the book of Acts. It all came from that one Jerusalem congregation.

Jesus' social action leads His church right into the same action. Many of His miracles were social-action miracles. They were not only acts of compassion and mercy. They were associated with the kingdom of God, redemptive.

He gave to the poor (John 13:29), but He did not feed all the poor in the land. He healed many, sometimes all, but He did not empty out every hospital nor did He heal every blind person in the country. He did not repeat His miracles in the same way every time. His usual way was to bless the usual. He did not always walk on the water. He usually made use of a boat. He did not always catch a fish with a coin in it to pay His taxes. He usually had Judas pay out of the treasury of their common purse, a purse largely kept in supply by women, such as He had healed of infirmities and unclean spirits (see Luke 8:1-3). He did not always provide loaves and fishes for the hungry. His works were not in the charity or welfare class. They were *works of God*, redemptive acts.

When He healed the man with the palsy, He also forgave his sins. At this, His critics became wild with rage, because this made clear to them that Jesus was performing a redemptive act of God.

The church ministered in His name. To a forty-year-old crippled beggar Peter and John said, "Look on us." He did, expecting to receive a handout. But Peter said, "Silver and gold have I none; but such as I have give I thee: in the name of Jesus Christ of Nazareth rise up and walk" (Acts 3:4ff.). Immediately he was made whole: his body was healed, his soul saved, and his poverty helped. It was another of Christ's redemptive acts through His church, for back of Peter and John there was a mighty assembly, accounting for the triple cure.

Three times we read of Jesus being angry. In each case, His anger was stirred not by personal insults or affronts but by actions which would hinder His doing good and helping others.

Another characteristic of the Jerusalem congregation was

that they "had all things common" (Acts 2:44), none lacked (see Acts 4:34), and they "shared with all men, as every man had need" (Acts 2:45). This all seemed to amplify the church's power and evangelistic thrust, because we read, the Lord kept on adding to the church "daily," those who were being saved (see Acts 2).

Barnabas demonstrated how widespread the blessing could be when he sold his land in Cypress and put all the proceeds in the church's common treasury (see Acts 4).

Ananias and Sapphira his wife, members of the Jerusalem church, cheated and lied about their property and possessions. By the power of the Spirit, Peter said: "Why has Satan filled your heart to lie to the Holy Spirit?" Two sudden funerals filled the entire assembly with the awe of God. Divine lightning struck this pair. A careful reading of Acts 5 makes it clear that this scene took place within the assembly. This first act of church discipline centered in the area of the social. It was assembly-action.

In chapter 6, this congregation faced a new problem in the social area: murmuring among the Grecians because "their widows were neglected in the daily ministration." What was to be done? Forget them and just "get on with preaching the gospel"? No, rather do two things: feed them *and* preach. Both were done, redemptively. Never did the apostles minister better or more effectively. Now they could "give themselves continually to prayer, and the ministry of the word" (Acts 6:4).

In many lands today, if we do not help the poor and sick and suffering, we do not earn the right to preach to them. We have no entrance. But there is a dimension which opens the door. Why do this "out there" and not here at home? All kinds of social action, rightly done, turn into church growth. The many facets of human brokenness open up a wider lane of light for Christ's love. One sunbeam, it is true, has all the colors of the rainbow in it. But these are not seen unless it rains. The light of Christ, shining through His church on the full spectrum of human need, is as beautiful as it is powerful.

HETEROGENEOUS BODY

The advance and growth in the Jerusalem church were more than geographical and historical. The congregation developed from a homogeneous into a heterogeneous body, at home in every race and culture and nationality. No darkness can put out its light. Darkness is a place for it to shine. It relates equally to a Samaritan and an Ethiopian. Soon, across the Taurus Mountains, the church would embody a lot of mixed blood: native Galatians, Phrygians, Jews, Greeks, Romans, slaves, army officers, and soldiers. Human family life and relations also became powerful social strata for church growth and structure.

Though often counter to Christ, the community is our point of contact for Him. We must never lose the "sinner contact" and rapport. Yet we dare not compromise the gospel or its Christ.

The more difficult task is to adapt and apply the gospel without compromise. Like Paul, we must be all things to all men, that by any means we may save some.

Christ is always contemporary. It is not easy for the church to keep pace with Him in this. Like Him, His church is both in contrast to and in continuity with its community, in the world but not of it.

Man is a two-way street. There must be reciprocal action—response. This focuses part of the tension between the "haves" and the "have nots." For instance, are people willing to work, or do they just want handouts? If the rich are not to exploit the poor, neither are the poor to exploit the rich. Christ does not set one class against the other. The "down and out" as well as the "up and out" must be "poor in spirit." Genuine poverty is one thing, but poverty resulting from sloth is another thing. It was no lazy beggar that Peter lifted and healed and helped at the Temple gate Beautiful. Jesus' hands were as busy as His feet and lips, but those He healed and helped were active and were also willing to get going with Him.

The more we move around in Acts, the more we realize we are in the midst of a massive amount of new power. The church takes over. *Assembly power dominates.* The local congregation is the basic unit for all the manifold action of the Holy Spirit. This is constantly seen in the Jerusalem congregation, no matter what the action is.

First, the entire assembly is called to prayer. Prayer meetings are launched into orbit and they launch the church into orbit. They become the most powerful meetings of the congregation, setting a new pattern for the new church.

THE FULLNESS OF THE SPIRIT

With respect to *power*, the entire congregation partakes of the fullness of the Holy Spirit and becomes "charismatic"—having all the gifts and graces of the Spirit in operation.

Today, speaking in tongues is heralded in many churches. In the Jerusalem church, *all* the gifts of the Spirit were present, including wisdom and faith and discernment. These gifts are less flashy, but of utmost importance. Wisdom is not ecstatic or exciting, so this gift receives little attention. Yet it is the leading gift of the Spirit. Who ever highlights the gift of faith? Peter demonstrated prophecy and its superior power in his preaching. But tongues is the one gift which surfaces today, and it can easily be overemphasized. This gift did not take over or decide any issues or direction in the Jerusalem congregation. The Holy Spirit operates in a much fuller dimension of power as He "congregationalizes" *all* the gifts and graces.

Witnessing in the Jerusalem congregation became corporate action. The whole witnessing process is amplified and becomes much more alive and colorful when it is the program of the congregation. This sets the pattern for all great awakenings and revivals.

The same kind of congregation-power was demonstrated in the work of *missions*. There was no dichotomy between evangelism and missions abroad. There was no "home" and "foreign" ministry. The church in Jerusalem reached out in both directions.

This organic congregational growth principle holds true all the way in preaching, teaching, and training. The Lord is "in the midst" of His church as promised—walking, talking, working there.

Social action is also congregational. Many of the gifts of the Spirit are social-action gifts, and we do not need to have "hang-ups" about this.

Where is the problem? It is not with the gospel, it is with the church. The church is social in its action—so is man. The social action of the church is nothing less than its Christ-action in the community.

The church in Acts gives us the right discernment. It is not the gospel which is weak—it is our church. The gospel is still the same gospel and Christ is alive. But our churches are dimming the light of Christ.

Our Christ becomes too small when our doctrine of the church is too small. The Jerusalem church suffered bodily because it ministered bodily, just as Christ did. And we are to be as He is in this world (see 1 John 4:17).

Some time ago a well-known church in Hollywood began to get involved in its "Jerusalem," covering an area within a mile radius from its location. "This was the mission field we had avoided," said one of the pastors. Members began to move down from the bleachers to the field. They began to invade the world and not avoid it. They became a force for Christ in the pockets of sin and vice and poverty. They found themselves knee-deep in new discoveries and developments.

THE FIRST STEP

Prayer was the first step, the "get involved" kind. Some members began to concentrate in prayer on certain buildings—a store, a supermarket, a medical center, a drug area, a "massage parlor." They also got the police involved. After some months, crime dropped six percent where it had been the highest in the nation. Massage parlors dropped from sixty-seven to twenty-two. Street prostitution began to be reduced markedly. The prayers of the church began to "bite in." Astonishing conversations took place, and many were added to that church.

Christians went to work on challenges *from a kneeling position and saw changes* in the area. "All had been so futile because we had given up in prayer," one leader said.

The converts from these needy spots were not only converted

to Christ but were added to the church, because they were won through the church. The more a church is involved in its community, the more Christ can change the community. The "communion of saints" is drawn from the communion of sinners!

In Los Angeles, there are prayer groups called "Christians in Government." Among them are the chief of police, judges, lawyers, and civic leaders. They work in a hard place—downtown Los Angeles—but they meet regularly to pray. And they are asking for prayer from the churches.

"We wish we could get our pastors involved," some say. "We wish we could get them to see what is really going on—the violence, immorality, the rotten politics, homosexuality, lesbianism, prostitution, organized crime, and so on. We are ashamed to talk about some of the things." The involvement they really want is the involvement in intercession. They feel the ministers are walking by "on the other side," as did the priest and Levite.

Christians sometimes think that the "separation of church and state" absolves us from involvement in our city and government. Christ happens to be head of both. He is even now "head over all things to the church which is his body, the fullness of him that filleth all in all" (see Ephesians 1). Right now He is "King of kings and Lord of lords" and "prince of the kings of the earth" (Revelation 1:5). He has "all authority in heaven and on earth" now (Matthew 28:18). His throne rules over all thrones, even *now*. That must mean, in a higher sense, that church and state are not so separate. In any case, prayer reaches to both—as does His throne. Intercession is earnestly enjoined for "kings and all who are in authority" (1 Timothy 2:2). So we must get our churches involved in this kind of prayer action. In all of these social action fields, is this the least thing we can do? No, it is the greatest!

A church I know of in Texas has developed a very busy and exciting ministry of prayer for every kind of need that comes to their attention. It even built a special prayer chapel for this new ministry. Requests are mailed in, phoned in, brought in. As a result, doors to all kinds of ministry are opening because people are finding answers to their needs through prayer. More people are being converted through this means than through visitation programs. It has become their most powerful evangelistic outreach.

What can we do? Every church does not need to build a special prayer chapel, but what about every church developing a prayer room ministry? Certainly our Lord gives prayer a high priority: "My Father's house shall be called a house of prayer." Every congregation should shape up a *prayer training plan*, a class which meets regularly. The pastor could lead it and all learn together.

With this training, begin a prayer room ministry and relate to all the concerns of the congregation and community. This same training group should help the pastor build up prayer in every direction: church, homes, special groups.

The Jerusalem congregation challenges us to make every

congregation a praying congregation, every member a prayer meeting member, every Christian a praying Christian—and every church and member, one involved in social action.

For whenever God is about to do any kind of a work, He always begins with prayer.

CHAPTER EIGHT

Epilogue—Assembly Power Principles

The Jerusalem church highlights some mighty important first principles concerning the dynamics of assembly-action. They are all functional and practical, like the laws of energy. Let's have a closer look.

THE FIRST TRUTH

What is the very first truth, the first fundamental about an "assembly"? What must be there before we even begin to speak about its action?

The very first thing about an assembly is that it must assemble! It is so obvious as to be embarrassing! This is basic. Primary. A *must*. To miss this is to miss the woods for the trees.

There is no way we can have assembly-action without first assembling. We can have action, but it will not be assembly-action. There is no way I know of that we can have assembly-power without assembling. We can have power, but not assembly-power. The very first thing we read of that congregation is that "when the day of Pentecost was fully come, they were all with one accord in one place" (Acts 2:1). They were assembled.

Somewhat later came the earnest admonition: "Not forsaking the *assembling* of ourselves together, as the manner [habit] of some is; but exhorting one another: and so much the more as ye see the day approaching" (Hebrews 10:25). This is one of the many urgencies that pulsate through the letter to the Hebrews. There is a sense now in which we can almost "*see* the day approaching."

Then are we to assemble less now, or more? Churches today are not so much forsaking doctrine as forsaking assembling. It is one of the most serious problems in bringing about church renewal. I said to a congregation: "If you do not assemble faithfully, you will soon cease to be an assembly."

In the Communist party, it has been said, absenteeism is treason. On the other hand, one of the first moves the Communists make is to break up the assembling of Christians. They know the power of an assembly! They maximize the forces of their own mass meetings. While they know the tremendous force inherent in the smaller cells, for total power and performance, they step up their mass demonstrations.

While multiplying all kinds of group and cell action, churches realize that the mighty works of God in revival are brought forth in mighty congregation meetings. I never heard of a great revival without great meetings. Pentecost set the pattern.

THE SECOND TRUTH

A second great truth about "assembly" is this: *not only some, but all the members are to assemble at those times when the assembly is called to assemble.* This is another fundamental principle, highlighted plainly in the Jerusalem assembly (see Acts 2:1). *All* were assembled in one place.

Why all and not just some, or almost all? Because that is what an assembly is, whether it is an automobile engine, or a symphony orchestra, or a human body, or anything which can be called an assembly. This is the nature of an assembly. It must be complete.

For example, take a look at your automobile engine. Not many parts dare be missing. If even a spark plug is missing the whole engine would be "missing." That plug is an "individual member." A second look tells us more: it is needed for total engine performance. Assembly-action! It is designed that way.

An even better example is the human body. It too is an "assembly." Every member of it is even born assembled and ready at once for assembly-action. To get this pen in hand, I actually had to bring my entire body to this desk!

This congregational truth is very powerful and forms the basis of Paul's argument with regard to the "charismatic" action of the Holy Spirit (1 Corinthians 12–14). If one member suffers, all members suffer; if one rejoices, all are to rejoice. The body needs every member and every member needs the body. We bear one another's burdens. This is the law of Christ. We are "members one of another." "Now you are Christ's body, and each of you a limb or organ of it" (1 Corinthians 12:27, NEB). Paul is here talking about the operation of spiritual gifts *when the members are gathered in assembly.*

It all sums up like this. The *Holy Spirit* is an assembly Spirit, just as my spirit is in me for body action. The same is true of the *risen Christ.* In one sense, He is far too great for any individual Christian to indulge in just by himself. He needs a body for all of His life and lordship and headship—the *church.* There are larger blessings which He has reserved for His assembled people, where He has promised to be present "in the midst." He is even now "head over all things to the church, which is his body, the fulness of him that filleth all in all" (Ephesians 1:22-23).

THE THIRD TRUTH

A third truth, or principle, of assembly-action is this: *Just as soon as I assemble with other Christians, my whole being goes into assembly-action.* This is true whether I think about it or stop to analyze it. As a person I begin at once to relate to the others present. A new kind of give-and-take attitude governs me. I defer, yield, and am considerate of the others gathered.

I become something like that spark plug in my engine. The moment I turn on the ignition, that plug begins to get going into engine action. It is not on its own. It lives and works for and with the assembled "members" of its "assembly."

The gasoline in the gas tank operates that way, too. And so does the oil in the crankcase. Together, they illustrate the working of the Holy Spirit in a congregation. The gasoline tells of the power and the oil demonstrates the *graces* in a meeting or in a Christian.

The firing system of God's Spirit is enormous in a congregation when all the members are present, pulling together in prayer, in love, and in the power of His Word.

THE FOURTH TRUTH

A fourth principle is this: *In assembly-action, the individual members do not cease to be strong as individuals.* They become stronger. They discover themselves. The whole personality flowers fully. The larger fellowship helps each to become self-conscious in the right way. By losing his life in others, he "finds" himself. Why is this? Because that is the way God made us. A great star on a ball team does not lose his personality or individuality because he is a member of the team. Rather, the team and all the teamwork bring out his individual performance and make him a star. He becomes total. The team peps up the star as much as the star peps up and inspires the team!

Not one member of a team plans to miss a single game in the whole year's schedule. He wants to be present and be at peak performance in every game. What a lesson for us in the church!

The measure in which members fail to assemble spells the measure of the leakage and loss of its *power in assembly.*

THE FIFTH TRUTH

This highlights another very powerful principle which has to do with revival. It is what we can call the *Law of Revival:* (a) The Holy Spirit works in the unconverted in proportion to His power and working in the converted. (b) The measure of conviction which the Holy Spirit works in the non-Christians is directly in proportion to the amount of burden Christians have for them.

Jesus spells this out very clearly in that classic on the Holy Spirit in John 16:7-11: "When he is come [*to you* as believers], he will reprove [convict] the *world* [unbelievers] of sin, and of righteousness, and of judgment" (italics mine).

This is precisely what happened in that most dynamic and dramatic of all awakenings, at Pentecost. When that day came, the Holy Spirit was not poured out promiscuously over the city of Jerusalem. Rather, He was given first to the assembled congregation, filling and firing its total membership. *Then*, and *through* them, plus Peter's preaching, thousands of unconverted Jews also assembled and were literally stabbed (pricked, pierced, convicted) in their hearts and cried out, "What shall we do?" Singly and in mass they repented—thousands of them—and the same day there were added unto them (the 120) about 3,000! *Jews*, mind you, most all of them. Who would even have dreamed it possible?

The record of it is now divine revelation—telling how much God can do in and with and through even one small congregation.

Mass power generates mass production. The new mass is the congregation on fire, and 120 members suddenly become 3,120.

Did this Jerusalem church realize it would get into the Bible and become part of the very Word of God—live on and on to become the standard-bearer of Christ's church everywhere on earth?

Charles Finney discovered this "law of revival." He described it this way: "When the *churches* are thus awakened and reformed, the reformation and salvation of sinners will follow, *going through the same stages of conviction, repentance, and reformation.* Their hearts will be broken down and changed. Very often the most abandoned profligates are among the subjects. Harlots and drunkards and infidels and all sorts of abandoned characters are awakened and converted. The worst of human beings are softened and reclaimed, and made to appear as lovely specimens of the beauty of holiness" (italics mine).

J. Wilbur Chapman, another of our country's leading evangelists, discovered the same "law" when he wrote: "The reason the unsaved do not attend is largely the fact that Christians have forsaken the services themselves, *and it is always a principle that the unsaved are only as much concerned for themselves as the saved are concerned for them*" (italics mine).

Plenary power is reserved for the gathered people of God. Fragmented assembling shreds it. As fire exists by burning and rain reaches us by raining, so the mighty power of an assembly comes about through assembling.

Our Mission:

"To stimulate an awareness of the necessity for prayer in the revival of the Church of Jesus Christ."

Our Methods:

Schools of Prayer—Bringing community pastors and churches together for two to three days to learn more about prayer from the Holy Scriptures; spending time in repentance, worship, praise and intercession that results in restoring their friendship with Christ, reviving their prayer life and impacting their community with Jesus' love and compassion.

Prayer Retreats—Enabling pastors and spouses to get away for two or three days at a scenic location for a time of renewal of mind, heart and body with an emphasis on prayer. At the present time the Northern Plains Prayer Retreat for ministers and spouses is held the third week in February in Medora, ND.

United Prayer Gatherings—Encouraging, uniting and preparing the Church of Jesus Christ for a genuine movement towards revival and spiritual awakening, featuring outstanding revival speakers.

Missions Outreach—Ministering and teaching in foreign countries in conjunction with other evangelical mission agencies that involve outreach in prayer summits, colleges and churches.

REVIVAL
PRAYER
FELLOWSHIP

For more information go to:
revivalprayerfellowship.com

*Prayer*CONNECT

A QUARTERLY MAGAZINE DESIGNED TO:

Mobilize believers to pray God's purposes for
their church, city and nation.

Connect intercessors with the growing worldwide prayer movement.

Equip prayer leaders and pastors with tools
to disciple their congregations.

Each issue of *Prayer Connect* includes:

- Practical articles to equip and inspire your
  prayer life.
- Helpful prayer tips and proven ideas.
- News of prayer movements around the world.
- Theme articles exploring important prayer topics.
- Connections to prayer resources available online.

Print subscription: $24.99
(includes digital version)

Digital subscription: $19.99

**Church Prayer Leaders Network
membership: $35.99** (includes print,
digital, and CPLN membership benefits)

SUBSCRIBE NOW.
www.prayerleader.com/membership or call 800-217-5200